Vet On Call

DOG CARE
Companions

Vet On Call

The Best Home Remedies for Keeping Your Dog Healthy

From the Editors of

part of the family™

Edited by Matthew Hoffman

Veterinary consultant: Christine L. Wilford, D.V.M., is a veterinarian in private practice in Seattle, Washington, and the "Veterinary News" columnist for *American Kennel Club Gazette.*

Rodale Press, Inc.
Emmaus, Pennsylvania

Notice

This book is intended as a reference volume only, not as a medical manual. The information given here is designed to help you make informed decisions about your pet's health. It is not intended as a substitute for any treatment that may have been prescribed by your veterinarian. If you suspect that your pet has a medical problem, we urge you to seek competent medical help.

Library of Congress Cataloging–in–Publication Data

Vet on call : the best home remedies for keeping your dog healthy / edited by Matthew Hoffman.
        p.   cm. — (Dog care companions)
   Includes index.
   ISBN 1–57954–225–5 hardcover
   1. Dogs—Diseases—Treatment. 2. Dogs—Health. 3. Dogs—Behavior.
I. Hoffman, Matthew. II. Series.
SF991.V424 1999
636.7'089—dc21   98–31657

Distributed to the book trade by St. Martin's Press
2 4 6 8 10 9 7 5 3 hardcover

┌─ OUR PURPOSE ─┐
**To explore, celebrate, and stand in awe
before the special relationship between us
and the animals who share our lives.**

Vet On Call

CONTRIBUTING WRITERS

Janine Adams, Bette LaGow, Kristine Napier,
Audrey Pavia, Christine L. Wilford D.V.M.

RODALE HEALTH AND FITNESS BOOKS

Editor: Matthew Hoffman
Vice-President and Editorial Director: Debora T. Yost
Executive Editor: Neil Wertheimer
Design and Production Director: Michael Ward
Research Manager: Ann Gossy Yermish
Copy Manager: Lisa D. Andruscavage
Cover Designer and Design Coordinator: Joanna Reinhart
Associate Studio Manager: Thomas P. Aczel
Book Manufacturing Director: Helen Clogston
Manufacturing Manager: Mark Krahforst
Manufacturing Coordinator: Melinda B. Rizzo

WELDON OWEN PTY LTD

Chairman: John Owen
Publisher: Sheena Coupe
Associate Publisher: Lynn Humphries
Senior Editor: Janine Flew
Project Editor: Kathy Metcalfe
Copy Editor: Lynn Cole
Senior Designer: Kylie Mulquin
Designer: Jocelyne Best
Illustrators: Virginia Gray, Chris Wilson/Merilake
Icons: Matt Graif, Chris Wilson/Merilake
Indexer: Garry Cousins
Production Manager: Caroline Webber
Production Assistant: Kylie Lawson

Film separation by Colourscan Co Pte Ltd, Singapore

CONTENTS

PART THREE

GIVING LONG-TERM CARE *113*

PART FOUR

SOLVING BEHAVIOR PROBLEMS *135*

Introduction

Dogs hate going to the vet. Reassuring words and friendly people don't disguise the fact that your vet's office is full of scary smells. Unfamiliar people and cold instruments. The indignity of getting their temperature taken. Any sensible dog would just as soon stay home—or at least do everything possible to avoid getting out of the car.

I once had an elderly Labrador, Rosie, who was calm, sweet-tempered, and well-behaved—until we pulled into our vet's parking lot. Rosie couldn't see very well, but she knew perfectly well that she didn't want to be there. Her usual strategy was to jump into the back of the car and attempt to hide, all 105 pounds of her, under the front seat. Her tail always gave her away, but she never quit trying. She felt safer back there and would put up quite a struggle in order to stay put.

Fortunately, Rosie was a healthy dog and we rarely had to make the trip more than once or twice a year. But I found myself wondering if it would be possible to treat many simple problems at home and save her that unnerving trip

to the vet. As I soon discovered, veterinarians were thinking the same thing. Which is why more and more vets have begun recommending—and teaching their clients to use—home remedies.

The simple truth is that home care is often the best care. For one thing, taking dogs to the vet is stressful, and stress can weaken immunity and slow the time it takes them to heal. Using home remedies means your dog is in familiar surroundings with people she loves and trusts. She still won't like having her temperature checked or her nails trimmed, but she's unlikely to panic, either.

But the main reason vets recommend home remedies is because they work. The term "home remedies" may sound old-fashioned, but veterinarians actually use these remedies every day—although they often call them by scientific names just to sound fancy. Take vinegar. It's very effective for controlling yeast and other organisms that cause skin infections. Vets use vinegar all the time—although the bottle it comes in probably says "acetic acid." It's essentially the same thing.

Hydrogen peroxide to clean wounds. Contact-lens solution (saline) to soothe sore eyes. Colloidal oatmeal to ease itchy skin. These and hundreds of other home remedies have been used for a long time. Veterinarians have found they often work just as well—or better—than "modern" veterinary products.

The editors at *Pets: Part of the Family* spent nearly six months interviewing the country's top veterinarians and animal behaviorists. Our goal was to discover exactly how to use home remedies to treat over 50 common concerns, in-

cluding behavior problems and long-term (and potentially serious) conditions such as arthritis, diabetes, and overweight.

Did they come through! The vets we talked to did a lot more than recommend specific remedies and techniques. They also shared their years of wisdom and experience (and some really great stories) and told us exactly how to use home care to get the best results. How to give a checkup at home. The best way to give an itch-relieving bath. When to use dips and when to use sprays. How to take a temperature or give a pill. And much more.

Some problems, of course, always need a veterinarian's care. Since it's not always easy for owners to tell which problems are "safe" and which are scary, we asked the experts to create a special feature, "Call for Help," which tells exactly when you need to call your vet for advice.

Most of the time, you will be able to treat your dog at home. Home remedies aren't a substitute for seeing your vet, but they're a wonderful complement: When you know what to look for and are confident treating common problems, you'll also find yourself catching potential illnesses at the earliest possible time. This means that you and your vet will be able to keep your dog healthier than ever. And there's nothing old-fashioned about that.

Matthew Hoffman

Matthew Hoffman
Editor, *Pets: Part of the Family* books

PART ONE

The Best Care Begins at Home

A dog's health and well-being are best maintained by the person who loves and knows her best—you. And the best place for this caring and commitment to take place is in the home she shares with you. When you learn to manage your dog's health you'll be giving her the best present she could ever hope to have.

CHAPTER ONE

WHY VETS RECOMMEND HOME REMEDIES

There are many home remedies that veterinarians respect and recommend—not only for common health problems like cuts, vomiting, and fleas, but also for behavior problems such as chewing and barking.

The moment you bring your dog home, the bond between you begins to form. As you work, train, and play together, you come to understand how your dog normally behaves and communicates. You can tell if he's feeling fine, or if he's not quite himself, with just one look. Most importantly, you grow to love and trust one another.

That, in a nutshell, is why when it comes to basic health care, you are often your dog's best vet as well as his best friend, says Bernadine Cruz, D.V.M., a veterinarian in private practice in Laguna Hills, California. Your observations, instincts, and understanding of your pet enable you to prevent illness, treat minor health problems, and provide your pet with a long life of good health, she says.

You can expect minor health problems throughout your dog's life, from cuts and scrapes to vomiting and dirty ears. These and many other problems are easily treated with home remedies, for example, putting mineral oil in your dog's ears to drown ear mites and reduce itching, or using tomato juice to rid your dog's coat of the smell of skunk spray. "Many pet owners don't realize how easy it is to carry out a number of health maintenance tasks and home remedies," says Dr. Cruz.

The Comfort of Home

Dogs that are seriously ill or injured, of course, always need a vet's care. But for minor injuries and ailments, treating your pet at home is not only less expensive and more convenient, it may even help your pet get better faster.

This Old English sheepdog-Border collie-cross is more relaxed being treated by his owner than he would be in the veterinarian's office.

"More than anyone else, your dog trusts you," says Dr. Cruz. He is accustomed to your touch, your voice, and your handling. He knows that when you're calm, it's okay for him to be calm, too. And when he's calm he's going to let you do things he's not particularly fond of, like trimming his nails, cleaning his ears, or treating minor cuts and scrapes. And he'll be a lot less stressed than if all these things were being done by a stranger, she says.

Another advantage of caring for your dog at home is that you don't have to make that trip to the vet, which in itself can be an alarming experience, says Peter Eeg, D.V.M., a veterinarian in private practice in Poolesville, Maryland. Your vet's office, no matter how comfortable the surroundings, is filled with unfamiliar sights and smells, as well as strangers. For dogs that are already sick, all the excitement can provoke even more anxiety. On top of that, dogs sometimes have unpleasant memories of past experiences, and just pulling up at your vet's office may bring those flooding back. "This can make it terribly difficult for your dog to cooperate with even minor procedures," says Dr. Eeg.

Since dogs are much more relaxed when they're in familiar surroundings, simple procedures like bandaging a cut are less likely to become major productions. Reducing stress has another benefit, as well. Tension and anxiety can raise your dog's heart rate, pump up blood pressure, and simply wear him out. In fact, the effects of stress can be almost as detrimental as whatever was bothering your dog in the first place. "In the long run, the trusting bond between you and your dog translates into the best health care," says Dr. Cruz.

A big part of home care is watching for behavior or energy changes that could be signs of health problems.

The Power of Prevention

One of the biggest advantages of home care is that once you know what to look for, you'll be able to detect signs of problems long before a vet ever could. After all, you spend hours together every day, while your vet probably sees your dog only once or twice a year. Since you know what's normal for your dog, you'll also know when things are a little "off."

You know how much enthusiasm your dog usually has when he greets you, how much he normally eats and sleeps, how hard he plays, and how he carries himself when he walks. Because you know him so well, you'll be able to detect slight changes in his behavior—and in his appearance—that might seem perfectly normal to your vet. "Early diagnosis is one of the critical factors in keeping minor medical problems from becoming major ones," says Dr. Eeg.

Knowing What's Normal

One of the best ways to know when something is wrong with your dog is to know what is right with him—in other words, what's normal. You gather a lot of information just by spending time with your dog. You'll gather a lot more when you check for specific things every day.

"Just in the process of cleaning your dog's ears, brushing his teeth, and brushing his coat, you can assess his health," says Diana van Tine, D.V.M., a veterinarian in private practice in Conifor, Colorado. If your dog's gums go from healthy pink to swollen red, for example, or you find bald patches in his typically healthy coat, you'll know right away that there is something wrong. (You'll learn more about home checkups on pages 13 to 19.) Obviously, the better you know your dog, the sooner you'll be able to catch potential problems. Here's a step-by-step plan for getting to know him a little bit better.

Walk him at least 10 minutes a day. "Pay attention to your dog's pep level and his interest in the world around him," says Dr. Eeg. For example, does he generally bound around the block with energy to spare, but one day he has to sit and rest? Is he suddenly making five pit stops instead of the usual one or two? Any change in his usual habits means that something could be going on, says Dr. Eeg.

Feed him the same food at the same time every day. Your pet should want to eat on a regular schedule and his appetite should be consistent, says Dr. Eeg. "When your pet begs for more food than usual or doesn't eat his usual fare for a couple of days, he could be sick."

Watch his water intake. Sudden changes in thirst—either drinking more or less—are often signs of serious illnesses. The only way to know when your dog's water intake has changed is to know how much he usually drinks. Dr. Eeg recommends measuring the amount of water you put in his bowl. This makes it easy to tell if he's drinking more or less than usual, and if you need to be concerned.

Know his routine. Does your dog always get up and greet the family first thing in the morning, looking for love and attention? "You might suspect something is brewing if he stays in bed long after the family has gathered in the kitchen," says Dr. Eeg.

This German shepherd loves to play and has plenty of pep. His owner will know right away when he isn't feeling quite himself.

This terrier-mix puppy loves his chew toy. A sudden loss of interest in a favorite toy could be a valuable warning sign that something's wrong.

Your Dog's Best Nurse

One of the benefits of taking charge of your dog's health is that you not only know when something's serious enough to merit a visit to the vet, but you'll also know which things you can handle yourself.

It takes a little time before owners feel comfortable giving health care at home—especially when they're faced with somewhat uncomfortable procedures, like trimming a dog's nails or wrapping a wound. But most health care, whether it's done at home or in your vet's office, isn't all that difficult when you know what you're doing. "Dogs are furry and walk on four legs, and that intimidates many people, but it shouldn't," says Steven Kasanofsky, D.V.M., a veterinarian in private practice in New York City. "Their health needs are basically pretty simple and easy. Most pet owners have far more ability than they give themselves credit for."

Thankfully, serious illnesses are rare. The types of problems you're likely to encounter are the ones you can easily deal with at home—for example, relieving the pain and itch of insect bites; draining blocked anal sacs; performing regular dental care (which can help you avoid expensive and uncomfortable dental cleaning at the vet's); cleaning dirty ears; treating diarrhea and vomiting; trimming cracked or splintered nails; and much more.

"It's very satisfying to take charge of your dog's health, and to prioritize his health problems and issues," says Dr. van Tine. "And when you are in charge, you will also know when you need to call your veterinarian for help."

Home remedies aren't meant to replace regular veterinary care, but to complement it, Dr. Eeg adds. As a bonus, the more you work with your dog at home, the more comfortable he'll be when it's time to see the vet. "As you care for your dog so lovingly during his minor medical problems and routine care, he learns that human touch is good—and is more likely to trust the veterinarian's touch when that becomes necessary."

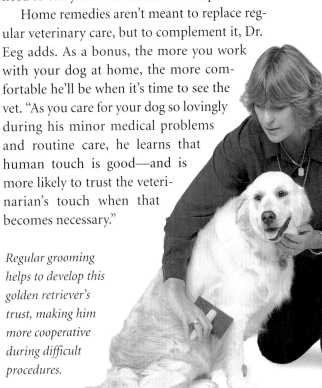

Regular grooming helps to develop this golden retriever's trust, making him more cooperative during difficult procedures.

5

When It's Time to Call the Vet

You can treat many problems at home, but some always require veterinary care, and some are emergencies. Get your pet to your veterinarian immediately if you notice any of the following:

- Difficulty breathing
- Severe vomiting or dry heaves
- Severe diarrhea
- Blood in stool
- Blood in vomit
- Severe bleeding
- Seizures or convulsions
- He's eaten chemicals or poisons
- Extreme weakness
- Persistent coughing
- Coughing up blood or other fluids
- Any kind of trauma. Even if your dog seems fine—after a car accident, for example—he could have internal problems that will quickly get worse without quick veterinary treatment.

Symptoms such as unusual discharges or odors, or a lack of appetite, should also be treated by a veterinarian, but they can usually wait until morning, says Dr. Eeg. "When in doubt, don't be afraid to call your veterinarian. If you have any uncertainty, then something is probably amiss."

Early Warning for Seizures

Thanks to the help of some very special dogs, people with epilepsy are now able to get a warning that a seizure is pending, allowing them to take precautions before it strikes.

Scientists have found that certain dogs have the ability to detect oncoming seizures five to 45 minutes before they happen. No one's sure how the dogs do it, but it's believed they detect subtle chemical or electrical changes in the brain, says Dave Monzo of Canine Partners for Life in Cochranville, Pennsylvania. This organization places these specially trained "seizure-alert" dogs with people who have at least one seizure a week.

"For people who suffer from seizure disorders, the biggest risk is getting injured when a seizure hits," Monzo says. The dogs can reduce this risk by whining and barking, letting their owners know that trouble's coming. This advance notice gives people time to sit down, move away from stairs, or otherwise get themselves into a safe place so that they don't fall down or hurt themselves while having a seizure.

The dogs do more than act like alarms, Monzo adds. They'll also lie close to—or even on—their owners during a seizure. This provides emotional comfort and also helps keep their owner's bodies stable, so they're less likely to hurt themselves while the seizure is occurring.

Even though these dogs receive a lot of training, you can't teach a dog to detect seizures. They have to have the ability in the first place—and not a lot of dogs have it. Those that have the ability, however, are easy to pick out of a crowd. "When you look in their eyes, you can feel the intensity and the focus," says Monzo.

PUPPY DOG TALES

CHAPTER TWO

TEACHING YOUR DOG TO BE A GOOD PATIENT

Through regular petting, handling, grooming, and training,
your dog will learn to trust your touch and she'll confidently allow you
and your vet to take good care of her.

Christine Wilford's dogs trust her so completely that she can stitch cuts, draw fluid from lumps, and perform many other uncomfortable procedures without giving them sedation. In fact, they're nearly the perfect patients—and it's not because she's a vet, says Dr. Wilford, D.V.M., a veterinarian in private practice in Seattle. It's because she's a good owner.

Most of us will never do the kinds of things with our pets that Dr. Wilford does with hers. And there aren't very many dogs who can undergo difficult procedures without complaining. In fact, a lot of owners despair when it's time to take their dog to the vet because they know she's going to struggle every inch of the way. These are the same dogs who won't hold still for checkups, who growl when you touch their paws or try to take their temperature, who won't let you give them a pill or do any of the other things you need to do to keep them healthy.

It doesn't have to be this way, says Dr. Wilford. Every dog can learn to put up with checkups, grooming, and the like without kicking up a fuss. But they do have to learn—it's not something dogs take to naturally. Formal lessons aren't necessary, Dr. Wilford adds. By teaching your dog some basic obedience and developing a deep and abiding bond, she'll naturally learn to trust you and all the other humans she's going to meet. In short, she'll become an ideal patient for you and your vet.

"Training your dog to obey and regularly grooming her at home will prepare her to calmly endure checkups and medical treatment," says Joan E. Antle, D.V.M., a veterinarian in private practice in Cleveland, Ohio. You may even find that some trips to the vet aren't necessary because your dog will trust you enough to sit calmly while *you* do the simple things that often need to be done.

This miniature schnauzer has learned to cooperate through regular handling and training.

Positive Handling

One of the most important lessons you can teach your dog is that hands—yours or anyone else's—are always friends, says Dr. Wilford. This is why veterinarians recommend never using hands to smack or discipline dogs, which can make them hand-shy. It's important for dogs to know that the hands coming toward them, no matter who's on the other end, always have a positive, loving intent—such as petting, feeding, grooming, stroking, and comforting. This will help your dog be more accepting of hands that have other, less pleasant duties to perform, such as examining, clipping, or bandaging.

Even when you're playing, you don't want to use your hands—or let your dog use them—roughly. Once she gets the idea that hands can be treated like toys, something to mouth or nip whenever she's excited, she'll be more likely to get rough at other, less appropriate times.

Basic Obedience

A dog doesn't have to be Lassie to be a good patient, but she should know the basics, like "sit," "stay," "down," "come," and "drop it," says Wayne Hunthausen, D.V.M., an animal behavior consultant in Kansas City. Dogs that are versed in basic obedience are much easier to handle when you need to do simple checkups, clean their ears, or anything else.

Dogs can learn obedience at any age, but they learn fastest and most easily when you start around three months. Training isn't a one-time affair, Dr. Hunthausen adds. Dogs need to practice, starting from the time they're puppies and continuing throughout their lives. "Think of your puppy as a toddler who needs consistency and practice at the rules of life," he says.

Older dogs can also learn the basic commands, he adds, although it may take them a little longer to develop new habits. You'll need to work with your dog for a few minutes every day, he advises.

Handle with Care

When you're training your dog, even simple things, done consistently, will have impressive results. This is especially true when you're teaching your dog to tolerate handling. The more you touch her, from the tip of her tail to the end of her nose, the more she'll trust—and appreciate—routine care.

A good place to begin is with simple grooming, says Dr. Wilford. Most dogs enjoy being stroked, and grooming is nothing more than a lengthy stroke session, except that you use a brush or comb instead of your hand. In the beginning, you may want to pass a brush lightly over your dog for a few seconds. As long as she holds still—and she probably will if you don't take too long—give her lots of positive feedback. It won't take long before she learns that the brush predicts good things to come.

While your dog is growing up—or while you're training an older dog—do a few minutes of grooming every day. Brush her coat. Trim her nails. Wipe sleepers from her eyes. The more touching you do, the quicker she'll get used to it, and, over time, the more she'll trust you.

This is also a good time to begin giving your dog a weekly checkup. Get her used to having you handle her mouth, neck, body, paws, and everything else you can reach. Your dog shouldn't have any trouble holding still for the five or 10 minutes this will take. See page 13 for more information on giving checkups at home.

One of the most important things is to get your dog used to having her mouth handled, says Dr. Antle. Veterinarians include a mouth exam as part of their regular checkups, and dogs that didn't have their mouths handled when young are unlikely to put up with it later on.

It's usually not difficult to teach dogs that mouth exams aren't a miserable experience. Begin by regularly opening her mouth and taking a quick look at her gums and teeth. This doesn't come naturally to all dogs, and it may take some time before she'll let you do it without fighting. But it's worth doing because many types of home care, from caring for the teeth to reaching into her mouth to retrieve a bit of stick, will involve having your hands in her mouth.

Your dog will probably struggle or possibly even

MUZZLING YOUR DOG

No matter how well-trained and cooperative your dog usually is, fear and pain can make her bite. That's why vets recommend starting first aid or emergency care by muzzling your dog first. (Don't muzzle a dog that's vomiting, has facial injuries, or is having trouble breathing.) You can buy muzzles from pet supply stores, or you can fashion one quickly from a leash, a necktie, or even a pair of panty hose. Here's how to do it.

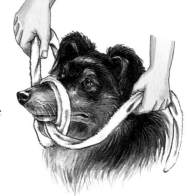

1 Tie a loose knot in the middle of the leash to create a large loop. Slip the loop over your dog's snout, pull it about halfway up the nose, and draw it tight.

2 Bring the ends down and knot them under your dog's chin.

3 Carry the ends behind the back of the ears and make a knot.

snap when she's first getting use to being handled. Resist the urge to hold her down or force her to comply. Force doesn't work and it makes dogs distrustful. A better approach is to take the time to teach her to sit or lie down, and remain still voluntarily. "I trained my Doberman to lie down on his side for his teeth cleanings," says Dr. Wilford. "He was so comfortable that he would fall asleep in my lap."

Use Your Voice Wisely

Dogs don't understand language the way we do, but they're exquisitely sensitive to the sounds of our voices. The minor lilts and dips tell them when we're proud or disappointed. Our voices also tell them when we're upset and nervous—and whether they need to be nervous too. "Take advantage of the trust she has in your voice during an illness or health emergency," says Dr. Hunthausen. No matter how upset you are,

This cocker spaniel has learned that when her owner sounds calm, she can be calm too.

keep your voice calm and reassuring. As long as you sound calm, she will be calm too.

It's fine to be stern when you need to be, Dr. Hunthausen adds. In fact, you should sound stern when your dog isn't cooperating. Telling your dog "everything's just fine" when she's acting up will give her the idea that you approve of what she's doing. It doesn't matter if she's hurt or not. If she's not cooperating, tell her so. Order her to sit or lie down. As long as she trusts you she'll do what you ask—even if her natural instinct is to do something different.

"Teaching your dog to be cooperative is simply a matter of socializing her," says Dr. Hunthausen. "Not only will she be more likely to cooperate at critical moments, but she'll be a much better friend and companion."

Scooter's Gift

Karol Breitholl has diabetes and she can never predict when her blood sugar's going to crash. These terrifying episodes come out of nowhere, leaving Karol confused and dizzy. More than once she has passed out in her West Milton, Ohio, farmhouse.

Even though Karol can't predict her blood sugar levels, her dog, an eight-year-old spaniel-mix named Scooter, can. Karol can't say how he does it, but when her blood sugar begins to fall, Scooter is all over her, licking her face, jumping up and down, or crawling in her lap—anything to keep her awake enough so that she can grab a glass of orange juice or some candy.

On the rare occasions that Karol's blood sugar does drop in her sleep, Scooter instantly wakes up and makes sure Karol or her husband wakes up too.

PUPPY DOG TALES

CHAPTER THREE

COMMON SYMPTOMS YOU SHOULD LEARN TO RECOGNIZE

Your dog can't tell you in words that he's not feeling well, but his body will do the talking for him. Once you learn to recognize a few symptoms and signals, you'll know right away what's wrong—and what you need to do.

Dogs send us a lot of messages every day about the state of their health. Sometimes, we can interpret these messages very easily and are in no doubt about how to respond. At other times, though, we know that something's wrong, but we're just not sure what.

Most of the time, the symptoms we're seeing

Dogs are creatures of habit, so when he's not his usual self, you'll know to check on his health.

are common ones. Your dog may have the occasional day when he just doesn't seem himself. Or maybe he skips his dinner or seems a little less enthused when you get home.

"The acronym we used in veterinary school was ADR—'ain't doing right,'" says Michael Matz, D.V.M., a veterinary internal medicine specialist in private practice in Tucson, Arizona. "This is actually the most common symptom an owner can expect to see, but you needn't rush to your veterinarian every time your dog is a little off."

A good guideline is to imagine yourself with the exact same symptoms, and think about if and when you would seek medical attention, adds Taylor Wallace, D.V.M., a veterinarian in private practice in Seattle.

"In trying to decide what to do, one of the major parameters to consider is age," says Dr. Matz. An older dog that suddenly becomes less active may have more of an urgent problem than a younger dog that temporarily loses his pep. Older dogs have less reserve, and can become sick very quickly. Younger dogs tolerate relatively more illness for a little longer, he adds.

Another guideline for when to be worried is how quickly and how severely your dog becomes ill. "If he's very ill in just a few hours or within a single day, this is clearly more of an urgent concern than when a problem develops over weeks or months," says Dr. Matz.

Over your dog's lifetime you will encounter a lot of symptoms and you'll need to distinguish between those that need urgent attention and those that don't.

Ten Symptoms to Watch For

There may come a time when your dog is seriously ill. Often, the warning signs will come on quickly. Other times, there will be a slow build-up to the problem over a few days. That's where knowing what's normal for your dog and what's not will pay dividends, alerting you to changes before they become an emergency. However, if your dog displays any of the following symptoms, you must seek immediate help from a veterinarian.

• **Persistent or bloody vomiting or dry heaves.** Dry heaves can be a symptom of bloat, which occurs very quickly and is an extremely serious condition.

• **Sudden change of appetite or thirst.** These sudden changes could indicate a serious problem such as diabetes.

• **Rapid weight loss.** This can be a sign of heart failure, diabetes, or liver or intestinal problems.

• **Any kind of bleeding, especially in the urine or stools.** This could indicate a serious illness or trauma.

• **Significant change in urination habits.** This could signal kidney failure, an infection, or some kind of poisoning.

• **Confusion, staggering, or collapse.** Any of these symptoms may indicate heart problems, brain problems, high blood pressure, hormonal disorders, or that a poisonous substance has been consumed.

• **Difficult breathing.** This may be caused by a foreign body obstructing the airways, or by heart and lung problems.

• **Weakness, lameness, lack of coordination.** These could be a result of trauma, infection, or heart failure.

• **Sudden persistent whining or crying.** This indicates your dog is in pain and you'll want to call your vet.

• **Persistent diarrhea.** This could indicate a severe infection, poisoning, bowel injury, cancer, or an intestinal disease.

Scary-Looking Things That Aren't Emergencies

Some things look worse than they are and can often be treated at home, or at least can wait if you can't see your vet right away. And some "symptoms" are actually normal for dogs.

• **Reverse sneeze.** This sounds like a prolonged, repetitive snort. It's a strange thing to see, but it's entirely normal.

• **Occasional vomiting.** It's not unusual for a dog to vomit occasionally because of stomach upsets, eating too quickly, or eating too much.

• **Torn toenail.** Nails can get caught and torn on all manner of things. Torn nails bleed a lot, but are easy to treat at home or at the vet's.

• **Knee cap popped out of place.** This occurs mainly in small and miniature dog breeds. It looks much worse than it really is. You'll need to call your vet, but it isn't an emergency.

• **Tapeworm segments around the anus.** These look like short grains of white rice and can be a little alarming the first time you see them, but they are easy to treat with medication that you can get from your vet.

CHAPTER FOUR

THE REGULAR HOME CHECKUP

Keeping an eye on your dog's health is really no harder than
keeping tabs on your own. Once you know what to look for, you'll
know right away whether you need to be concerned.

You don't need a medical degree to know when you're sick. When your joints hurt, you've got a fever, and the only thing you want to do is sleep, you know you're in for a miserable few days. But it's not so easy to tell when dogs are under the weather. They're a lot more stoic than people. A dog can have a cracked tooth and happily continue chewing sticks and gobbling her food, without giving any sign that something's wrong.

Dogs can't tell us when they're sick or that an eye is sore, or they have an ear infection. And they usually don't respond to health problems the way we expect them to. That's why home checkups are so important. They give you a chance to discover small problems before they blossom into big ones. Of course, your veterinarian can catch plenty of health problems too—but he only sees your dog once or twice a year, and a lot can go wrong in between. Besides, you know your dog's habits and personality. You'll know right away when things aren't as they should be, and you'll have a pretty good sense of whether they're serious or not.

"You can check your pet's health so playfully and gently that she won't even know she's having an exam," says Joan E. Antle, D.V.M., a veterinarian in private practice in Cleveland,

Ohio. She recommends giving your dog a quick checkup, from the end of her tail to the tip of her nose, once a week. A checkup doesn't take more than five or 10 minutes, and your pet will enjoy the attention. And you'll enjoy knowing that nothing's going to slip by unnoticed.

The Checklist

You don't have to be a veterinarian to give a thorough exam, says Dr. Antle. You just have to know where to look—and what to look for.

Ears: Think Pink

Ear checks are important because dogs have a high risk of ear infections, says Merry Crimi, D.V.M., a veterinarian in private practice in Portland, Oregon. The problem is the way their ears are designed. There's a long tube that angles downward

Pricked-up ears, like these basenjis', are easy to check, while dogs with floppy ears take a bit more work.

from the opening. Where that tube ends a horizontal tube begins. This design helps protect the ear from injuries, but it also traps wax, leaves, and other debris that can make the ears just plain dirty—and prone to infection.

• Healthy ears should be smooth, glossy, and odorless, with a slight sheen of oil. They shouldn't contain anything but a little hair and a lot of pale, pink skin.

• When checking your dog's ears, use your nose as well as your eyes. "If you detect an odor, an infection could be brewing," says Dr. Crimi. Bright pink or reddened tissue inside the ear, or a black, yellow, green, or bloody buildup or discharge are signs of infection. A dark, waxy buildup, on the other hand, probably means her ears just need a good cleaning. For more information on cleaning the ears see pages 51 to 54.

• Dogs' ears trap more than grit. They also trap parasites, like ticks and ear mites. Ear mites are difficult to see, but they leave behind an abundant reddish-brown crusty discharge.

• Even if you can't see anything wrong, you should suspect ear problems if your dog is frequently scratching, tilting, or shaking her head. You should also be suspicious if the ears are unusually tender, or if your dog seems dizzy or is having trouble holding her head upright. These are signs of

This fox terrier has bright, clear eyes—the very picture of good health.

a serious ear infection and you'll need to call your vet right away.

Eyes: Clear and Bright

Eye exams are easy. All you have to do is stroke your dog's head. As you stroke her ears back, you'll be able to get a good look at her eyes.

• The eyes should be clear and bright, with a shiny, clear center. The pupils should be the same size, and the tissue under the lids should be a nice healthy pink. (Some breeds have a blackish tinge on the pink membrane.)

• Eyes that are red or filled with yellow or green pus almost certainly are infected. Heavy tearing also suggests an infection, although short-faced breeds like pugs and Pekingese always produce a lot of tears, which they need to keep their bulging eyes moist. These breeds also have a unique head construction that causes tears to run down their faces instead of along the tear canal, making them appear more weepy.

• If just one of the eyes is red, there's a good chance something's stuck in one of their three eyelids. "Nature gave dogs a third eyelid to protect them as they charge through brushes and brambles, and that's often where debris gets stuck," says Craig N. Carter, D.V.M., Ph.D., head of epidemiology at the Texas Veterinary Medical Diagnostic Laboratories at Texas A&M University in College Station. You can see the third eyelid as just an outline around the bottom of the eye. But most people never see it—until something's stuck in there. Then the third eyelid gets red, watery, and prominent, and your dog may need antibiotics.

• It's natural for a dog's eyes to change over time, says Nick A. Fabor, D.V.M., a veterinary

WHAT TO LOOK FOR

Start your dog's weekly home checkup by looking at her ears, then move on to the eyes, nose, mouth, body, limbs, tail, and paws. The examinations only take a few minutes, and your dog will enjoy the attention.

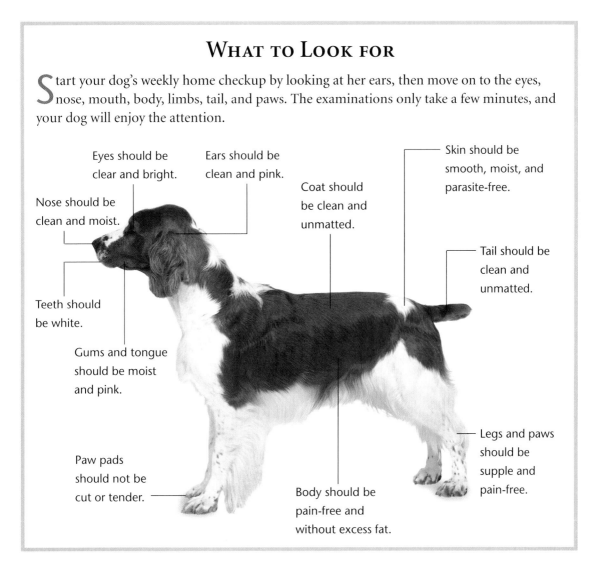

Eyes should be clear and bright.

Ears should be clean and pink.

Skin should be smooth, moist, and parasite-free.

Nose should be clean and moist.

Coat should be clean and unmatted.

Tail should be clean and unmatted.

Teeth should be white.

Gums and tongue should be moist and pink.

Legs and paws should be supple and pain-free.

Paw pads should not be cut or tender.

Body should be pain-free and without excess fat.

ophthalmologist at the School of Veterinary Medicine at the University of California, Davis. Some changes are normal, and others are not.

• One normal change is that the eyes sometimes take on a bluish cast as dogs get older. This happens as more and more discarded eye cells build up in the center of the eye, but it doesn't cause significant changes in vision, says Dr. Fabor.

• When the blue is accompanied by silver flecks or a cloudy cast, however, your dog could have cataracts, which is a hardening of the eye lens. A bluish eye that's also blood-shot or painful may signal glaucoma, a serious condi-

15

tion that may cause blindness if it isn't treated quickly. It's important to see your vet right away if you notice these changes. Glaucoma is most common in cocker spaniels and basset hounds.

Nose: Cold and Wet

A dog's nose doesn't say much about her health. A warm nose doesn't mean your dog is sick, any more than a cold nose means she's healthy. But it should be moist, not dry or cracked. There shouldn't be a discharge or loss of pigmentation.

Mouth: Fresh Breath, Clean Teeth

Many folks just assume that dogs have bad breath and dirty teeth. Nothing could be further from the truth. Your dog's teeth, all 42 of them, should be white and healthy. Her gums should be a bright, bubble-gum pink, maybe tinged with black, depending on the breed. And her breath shouldn't be offensive.

• Red gums and bad breath are early warnings of serious dental disease. "It's important to open up your dog's mouth regularly and take a peek," says Dr. Crimi. Catching problems early can prevent your dog from losing teeth later on.

• "While you're in there taking a look, brush your dog's teeth," advises Dr. Crimi. Dogs should get their teeth brushed every day, but a few times a week is usually enough to prevent problems.

Body and Limbs: Supple and Free from Pain

Feel along your dog's spine and gently apply pressure over her chest and abdomen. She shouldn't show any pain when you touch these areas. To make sure there isn't any stiffness or pain in your dog's legs, carefully lift them up one by one. Look for swellings, lumps, sores, or any other changes. Check your dog's posture for any rigidity or hunching.

A Healthy Heart Rate

A healthy heart rate for dogs is between 60 and 150 beats a minute, depending on their size. Generally, larger dogs have a bigger heart and therefore a slower heart rate than smaller dogs. Ask your veterinarian what the normal heart rate is for your dog.

• The best place to check your dog's heart rate is the femoral artery, which runs along the thigh bone on the inside of the hind leg, about halfway between the hip and the knee. You'll feel a distinct groove between the muscles there. That's where you want to place your fingers (don't use your thumb, which has its own pulse). Using gentle pressure, count the number of beats in 15 seconds. Multiply the number by four to get the number of beats per minute. Your dog's pulse should feel strong and fall within the normal range. If it is rapid, weak, or erratic, have your vet check it out.

Lungs: Easy Breathing

Using your ears is the best way to check your dog's respiratory health. If she's breathing normally, you shouldn't hear much of anything. Of course,

The femoral artery is the easiest place to check your dog's pulse.

your dog may snore in her sleep, but her normal breathing should be very quiet. Her breathing should be fairly slow and steady, about 10 to 30 breaths per minute.

• To check your dog's breathing, wait until she is lounging calmly or sleeping, then count the rise and fall of her chest as one breath. Count how many breaths she takes in a minute. If your dog seems breathless or her breathing is rapid while she's resting, have her checked by your veterinarian.

• Many conditions can cause changes in breathing, including allergies and heart disease. If she suddenly sits up and gasps for air, for example, that could be a sign of serious heart problems, especially if it's accompanied by coughing up fluid, and you should get her to a vet immediately.

• Dogs who become exhausted after normal exercise and pant excessively may have a respiratory problem or some other illness, and will need a checkup.

Circulation: Free and Clear

Healthy circulation ensures your dog is getting blood and nutrients pumped to all the places where she needs them. Though it sounds like a medical test, checking your dog's circulation is easy to do.

• Lift up your dog's lip from the side of her mouth and press firmly, but gently, on the gum above her sharp canine tooth. When you stop pressing, there should be a pale spot that becomes pink again within two seconds. If the spot remains pale for more than two seconds, your dog could have circulation problems and you should see your vet right away.

This collie-cattle dog-cross sits quietly while her owner checks her breathing.

Hair and Skin: Shiny and Clean

Your dog's coat and skin are excellent clues to her health. A healthy coat should be even, without patchy hair loss or thinning. Depending on the breed, healthy skin can be pink, brown, black, or spotted. It should be dry, pliable, and free of odors. There shouldn't be any dandruff, scales, bumps, excessive oiliness, or sores.

• It's easy to notice changes in your dog's coat by petting her regularly. But you should also part the hair with your fingertips and inspect her skin as well. "Pay special attention to several areas that tend to be troubled by skin and coat problems: Under the neck, belly, armpits, groin, the area over the knees and ankles, the area over the spine near the tail, and also the area around the anus," says Dr. Carter.

• Check that the hair around your dog's anus is clean and not matted, and is parasite-

free. "Bugs and insects—no matter what their size—are never normal and should alert you to a parasitic infection," says Dr. Carter.

Weight: Fit and Trim

Back when dogs ran wild, weight wasn't much of an issue, mainly because finding food kept them busy. Today, however, with the food bowl no more than a room or two away, packing on the pounds is a problem.

• Dogs that get too heavy start feeling uncomfortable. They also have a higher risk of getting diabetes and arthritis. Since dogs don't go from firm to fat overnight, it's important to check your dog's weight regularly to keep it from creeping up.

• You don't have to weigh your dog to find out if she's getting too heavy. You can do a quick weight check with your hands and eyes. Look at (and feel) her ribs. If you can't see or feel them, she's certainly overweight. Ribs that are too prominent, by contrast, could mean that your dog is underweight.

This miniature fox terrier is about the right weight. Her owner can feel the ribs, but they aren't too prominent.

Feet and Nails: Groomed and Comfortable

Your dogs toenails should just touch the ground, letting the toes stand together in a compact group. When they've grown too long, the nails cause the foot to spread out. This makes it difficult for dogs to walk comfortably or even normally—they have to change their gait to accommodate those spikes.

• It's important to keep the nails trimmed, says Dr. Crimi. Nails that grow too long often get snagged on rugs, floor cracks, or even on clothing. It's something to avoid because a torn nail can be nasty, bloody, and painful, Dr. Crimi says. See page 87 for more information on trimming your dog's nails.

• While you're checking your dog's feet, take a look between the toes. Look for hair mats, burrs, sores, or ticks. And check the pads for any sign of cracking or cuts.

Temperature: A Little on the Warm Side

Dogs make great bed warmers in the winter because their normal body temperature runs about 99.5° to 102.5°F—what we would consider a fever. But your dog's body temperature shouldn't be too warm because that could be a sign of infection or other health problems.

• When taking your dog's temperature, always use a rectal thermometer, which is less likely to break than the kind meant for oral use. Shake it down to below 99°F and lubricate it with petroleum jelly (vegetable oil works in a pinch). If you can, ask someone to hold your dog's head and shoulders and speak to her gently while you slide the thermometer in about an inch or two. Leave it in for two to three minutes to get a good reading. Then remove it, wipe it with tissue, and check the reading.

• You don't have to rush to your vet just because your dog has a slight fever, says Jillian Mesnick, D.V.M., a veterinarian in private practice in Mayfield Village, Ohio. It's not uncommon for dogs to run a little warm when they have a virus or some other infection. But a fever shouldn't last more than a day or two, says Dr. Mesnick. If it does, you'll want to call your vet for advice.

Daily Habits: Consistency is Best

One of the best indicators of your dog's health is consistency: She should eat, drink, and exercise about the same every day, and her bowel and urinary habits shouldn't change much, either. When any one of these elements suddenly changes, you'll know your dog isn't quite feeling herself and could be getting sick.

• "If your dog doesn't want to go outside to relieve herself, or if she can suddenly hardly wait to get out to her spot, or becomes incontinent, suspect a problem," says Dr. Carter. Urinary problems crop up with age and are often signaled by changes in urinary patterns. Similarly,

PUPPY DOG TALES

The Dog Who Loved Cats

It's not just people who love their pets. Some dogs have a natural instinct to take care of other creatures, too.

Sud Walters was driving home when she saw a sick-looking stray dog by the side of the road near her home in Darling, South Africa. She noticed that the undernourished, black dog was a nursing mother. Assuming that she had hidden her puppies, Sud searched the nearby bushes and found two bundles of black fur. She checked to make sure there were no others, then rushed all three animals home.

Sud gave the little ones the opportunity to nurse, and was very surprised when the "pups" started to purr. The dog, who had recently given birth, had been feeding and mothering two young kittens.

Sud contacted the animal rescue authorities, and the dog, newly named Emmy, was adopted by Rena and Dennis Hodson, of Bishopscourt, South Africa. Emmy was suffering from mange and an injured paw, but the Hodsons were thrilled to adopt her because they were so moved by her caring for the kittens when she was suffering herself.

Emmy left the kittens in the good care of the Domestic Animal Rescue Group, who bottle-fed them every four hours and found a home for them.

No one ever discovered, though, the answer to the intriguing mystery of how the three managed to come together.

bowel problems are usually signaled by changes in a dog's normal habits.

• Keep an eye out for changes in energy, as well. If your dog usually spends hours patrolling the backyard for squirrels, but one day entirely ignores the excitement, you can be pretty sure something's wrong and you'll want to take a second look. "Dogs are truly creatures of habit, so take seriously any change in your dog's daily routine," says Dr. Carter.

CHAPTER FIVE

A GUIDE TO HOME CARE

Most health problems are easy to treat at home once you know what to look for. And you don't need expensive equipment or specialized products. With practice and a few home remedies, you'll quickly discover how easy it is to keep your dog healthy.

Dogs are always banging into things and eating what they shouldn't. If you drove to the vet every time your dog got sick, you'd never have time to take him for a walk. "Spending a little time to learn about ways to handle minor problems and emergencies will give you the confidence to cope efficiently," says Bernadine Cruz, D.V.M., a veterinarian in private practice in Laguna Hills, California.

Home care isn't difficult, but it does require a little planning. First, you'll need to put together a first aid kit. Then, it's a good idea to build up a supply of items to help with all the little problems you're going to encounter, from coughing to minor cuts. Take a quick look in your cupboards, and you'll find you have some of the basics already.

Basic Home Remedies

There are many things at home that work well as simple home remedies.

- Baking soda. Sprinkle a little into your dog's bath to help relieve itching and sunburn.
- Peanut butter. This is a tasty treat that effectively conceals pills and capsules your dog may otherwise spit out.
- Citrus or cranberry juice. Mix a little of either juice into food to ease urinary problems.

- Cornstarch. This is very useful for dusting into skin folds to prevent chafing.
- Epsom salts. To help ease the sting of hot spots, sprinkle a little Epsom salts in the bath.
- Fabric softener. Put a capful of fabric softener in a bucket of water to give your dog a good final rinse after a bath. It removes the dander (saliva) that builds up on a dog's coat.
- Tomato juice. A thorough soak in tomato juice will help remove the odor of skunk spray.
- T-shirt. They are great for stopping dogs from licking and chewing at wounds.
- Vegetable oil. Sunflower or safflower oil stirred into food helps with dandruff.
- Yogurt. A little plain yogurt stirred into your dog's food helps restore the good bacteria in the digestive tract—a must after diarrhea.
- Aloe vera moisturizer. This is ideal for treating cracked paws and for soothing itches.

Human Medications that Will Work for Dogs

Some of the same treatments that work for humans also work for dogs. It's a good idea to talk to your vet before giving human medicines to pets, but the following are often helpful.

- Benadryl or Tavist. These antihistamines are good for treating hayfever.

FIRST AID KIT

Most people have a first aid kit well-stocked with adhesive strips, antiseptics, and other emergency care items. It's just as important to have one for your dog. Not only will you use it often for routine care—for cleaning your dog's ears, for example—but you'll also have at your fingertips everything you need to cope with unexpected mishaps.

VITAL INFORMATION CARD

Vet name and phone #

Emergency pet clinic phone #
address and travel directions to clinic

Veterinary poison control hotline phone #

- Dog first aid manual such as *Pet First Aid*

Critical Supplies
- A man's necktie made into loose noose (for a muzzle)
- Cotton balls
- Blunt-tipped tweezers

- Blunt-tipped scissors
- Needle-nose pliers
- Hydrogen peroxide (to induce vomiting)
- Syrup of Ipecac (also to induce vomiting)
- Large, needleless syringe to give liquid medications
- Eyewash (such as contact lens solution)
- Antibiotic ointment
- Rectal thermometer
- Antiseptic wash such as chlorhexidine or Betadine

- Gauze rolls
- 1 to 2 inch nonstretchable and stretchable gauze pads of varying sizes
- Packing and first aid tape
- Ace bandages
- Empty paper towel holder (for tail splint)
- K-Y jelly
- Chemical ice packs and hot packs

- Buffered aspirin. This eases the pain of arthritis. Give one-quarter of a 325-milligram tablet per 10 pounds of a dog's weight, once or twice a day, or as directed by your vet. Ascriptin, which is coated with Maalox, is even better for dogs than buffered aspirin.
- Triple antibiotic ointment. This is good for using on minor cuts, scrapes, and infections.
- Sunscreen. Buy a sunscreen with an SPF (sun protection factor) of 15-plus, and check that it does not contain PABA, a substance that can be harmful to dogs if they lick it off.

- Kaopectate. To quickly soothe stomach upsets, give one teaspoon for every 10 pounds of your dog's weight.
- Pedialyte. This is a quick-acting rehydration solution that replaces fluids after diarrhea.
- Metamucil. Sprinkle a little in your dog's food to help ease constipation and diarrhea.
- Pepto-Bismol. This is good for soothing stomach problems. Give one teaspoon per 20 pounds of your dog's weight, every 4 to 6 hours.
- Witch hazel. This cooling liquid eases the sting of bites, sunburn, and hot spots.

A Dog's Diary

One of the trickiest parts of health care is figuring out what causes symptoms to occur. Suppose your dog gets a rash every spring when the flowers start to bloom. Or he gets an ear infection after swimming in a pond. In such cases it's likely there is a connection, but it's not always easy to make that link between a health problem and its cause. That's why vets recommend keeping a pet-care diary.

"Keeping a diary about your pet's health can be a big help in figuring out how to treat problems in months and years to come," says Steven Kasanofsky, D.V.M., a veterinarian in private practice in New York City. "If your dog tends to get ear infections frequently, write down the type of infection and what your vet prescribed for treatment. You may start to see a pattern to those ear infections, and can then start to find ways to anticipate or prevent them from happening."

Once a year, your dog may come down with a bad case of itching. By checking the diary, you may realize that this usually happen in June—about the same time as your family vacations in a forest preserve. Put the clues together and you may discover that your dog has an allergy—to poison ivy, for example—that you never knew existed.

infected. Before you do anything, comfort your dog. You may need to muzzle him if he is distressed because he may bite. See page 9 for making a muzzle.

• Clean the injured area very gently. Use sterile pads and lots of warm, soapy water, says Lori A. Wise, D.V.M., a veterinarian in private practice in Wheat Ridge, Colorado.

• Once the wound is clean, rinse off all traces of soap with warm water.

• Dry the wound with sterile gauze pads. Avoid using cotton balls with open cuts because some of the fibers could stick and be hard to remove.

• Dry the surrounding fur with a clean towel.

• Apply an antibiotic ointment. Add more at regular intervals until the wound heals.

• Watch for any signs of infection. "These include redness, swelling, a nasty odor, or a discharge from the wound," says Dr. Cruz. See your vet if an infection does occur.

Most wounds will heal perfectly well if they're left open to the air. However, if your dog is addicted to trawling through mud, or insists on worrying the wound, it's best to apply a dressing, advises Dr. Cruz.

• Cover the wound with a sterile pad.

• Secure the pad with a roll of gauze. Tape the end of the gauze to the layer beneath.

Easy Home Procedures

Most health care doesn't require advanced training. In fact, the two procedures you'll use more than any others are also the simplest: Treating minor wounds and giving a pill. Here's what you need to do.

Wound Care

Due to their rough and tumble play, scrapes and cuts are a fact of life for most dogs. Minor wounds are easy to treat and usually don't get

• Repeat the procedure with white bandaging cloth. This will help stop moisture from getting in and will make it harder for prying teeth to dislodge.

• Change bandages at least every other day—more frequently if they get wet or dirty.

• Whenever you change the dressing, repeat the washing, rinsing, and ointment routine.

Giving Pills

You'll soon work out the pill- or capsule-giving technique that suits your dog best. Hiding it in food is one way to go. A dollop of peanut butter is great because dogs love it, and it's so sticky that they can't separate it from the medicine.

When your dog is ill and off his food, you'll have to work a little harder to make the pill go down. Gently maneuver him into a corner and have him sit up. With your left hand gently pull his upper jaw toward the ceiling.

Hold the pill between your thumb and finger and use the other fingers to push the lower jaw down. Put the pill near the back of the tongue. Then hold his mouth closed until he swallows.

The Learning Process

Taking care of your dog is an ongoing process, with each age and stage of his life presenting different challenges. Don't be daunted by the need to learn new techniques. On your visits to your veterinarian, ask him to explain and demonstrate any procedures you feel you should know. The more you expand your repertoire of home care, the better for both you and your pet.

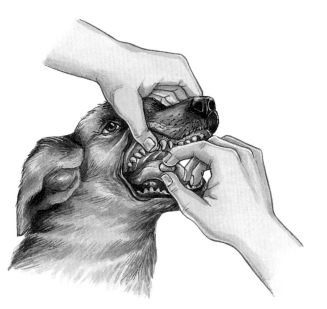

Place the pill between your thumb and finger and use your other fingers to push the lower jaw down. Put the pill near the back of your dog's tongue.

Hold your dog's mouth shut until he swallows. He may be reluctant to swallow, so gently massage his throat to encourage the swallowing action.

CHAPTER SIX

A Healthy Home for a Healthy Dog

Dogs don't err on the side of caution. They happily investigate all the exciting things life has to offer with never a thought to the consequences. You'll need to do a little thinking for them and make their home and surroundings as safe as possible.

A dog's middle name should be "inquisitive." Some aren't just curious, though, they're downright nosy. Add a dash of recklessness, and you have a combination that, while endearing, can also make your heart stop a beat now and then. While you don't want to dampen your dog's enthusiasm for life, you do want to make sure it doesn't get her into trouble. "Dogs gobble spilled medications and race out of open gates into traffic because they simply don't know any better," says Merry Crimi, D.V.M., a veterinarian in private practice in Portland, Oregon. That's why it's important to dogproof your home and its surroundings, much as you would childproof your house and yard.

Dogs are constantly using their mouths and noses to check out the world around them,

Dogs have more curiosity than common sense, so it's important to make sure your yard is securely fenced.

says Dr. Crimi. And they have a remarkable ability to get hold of—and into—things that we don't consider them capable of. A childproof cap on a bottle, for instance, is no obstruction at all to an inquisitive dog, and a cupboard that seems firmly closed can often be nosed open, given time and tenacity. And once they've gotten into what it is that interests them, dogs are unable to discriminate between what's good for them and what's not. Their natural urge will be to swallow their chosen object, which could be a pile of snail bait or a bag of potatoes.

It's important to remember that a smell or taste that would send a human reeling can have an irresistible appeal for a dog. It only takes one look at a dog blissfully rummaging through rotting garbage or rolling in dung to tell you that.

Creating a Safe Home

To make your house safe for your dog, you need to think like a dog. Consider your dog's habits and her response to different situations, and you'll be better able to pinpoint the danger zones and turn them into safe havens. The following tips will help you target the items and areas of your house you need to dogproof.

Lock away toxic materials. Toxic substances like dishwashing liquid, kerosene, and paint taste great to dogs. Make a quick survey of your house to remind yourself what you keep where, and how accessible it may be to your pet.

- Kitchen. Most kitchens typically have all sorts of cleaning products kept under the sink, some of which can be quite dangerous for your dog. Disinfectants and cleaners should all be locked securely away. Store them on a high shelf, if possible.

- Bathroom and laundry. Cleaners that are powerful enough to remove bathroom scum and molds can also remove the lining of your dog's mouth and throat. Bleach, clothes detergent, and fabric softener can all be toxic and must be locked carefully away. Make sure she doesn't drink the toilet water because it may have harmful bacteria or poisonous additives.

- Garden shed and yard. Gas, weedkiller, and pesticides, especially slug bait, are all dangerous for dogs. Make sure these products aren't accessible.

- Garage—Garages are filled with oil spills, sharp objects, and other accidents waiting to happen. It's best to just keep your pet out of the garage when you aren't around.

If you must temporarily house her there, take care to remove opened cans of paint, turpentine, or other toxic substances. And give the floor a careful wipe-up. Antifreeze is particularly attractive to dogs, so make sure you store it safely, and that it is not leaking from your car. Also, buckets of cleaning materials may look like drinking water to your pet, so never leave them unattended.

Keep medications out of reach. It may be convenient to keep your medication on the nightstand, but that means it's also convenient for your pet to get hold of them. Human medications are one of the major causes of poisoning in dogs, so it's critical to keep them out of reach. If you keep medicine in your purse, be sure it's zipped tightly at all times, adds Dr. Crimi. "Purses are one of the most common sources of medication poisonings." Also, be careful when taking medications because dogs quickly gobble dropped pills while you're not looking.

This Hungarian vizsla is indulging his natural curiosity with a sniff through his owner's purse— a good reason to keep handbags, which often contain medications, out of reach.

Secure electrical cords. To you it looks like an electrical cord. To your puppy, and maybe even to your adult dog, it may look like a rope toy. This sets up a potentially dangerous situation, since biting through an electrical cord can cause severe mouth burns and can even stop your dog's heart from beating, explains Paul Gigliotti, D.V.M., a veterinarian in private practice in Cleveland. Puppies are particularly prone to chewing and pulling at cords, and though they may grow out of it, some dogs never give up this habit. To be on the safe side, cover up or securely tape down all exposed cords.

Put away the people food. Rich human food, bones, and food hot from the oven all seem to act like magnets when a dog's around. "Some dogs who sneak a bite from just-cooked food suffer severe mouth burns, or can even choke on bites that are too big," says Ron Carsten, D.V.M., a veterinarian in private practice in Glenwood Springs, Colorado.

A dog' stomach can't cope with sudden changes in diet, which is why human food in unlimited quantities should be avoided.

Chocolate, in particular baking chocolate, contains theobromine, which is very dangerous for dogs.

Eliminate temptation by putting food out of reach, even if you're only leaving the room for a moment.

Keep the lid on the trash. Dogs are notorious trash-rummagers. Old food scraps or the residue in the bottom of a bottle of drain cleaner are all suitable menu items from a dog's perspective. Make sure your dog can't reach the trash, and that you keep all garbage cans tightly closed both inside and outside the house.

Put food out of your dog's reach. This Rottweiler is attracted by the aroma of the pizza, but it's hot and could burn her mouth.

Create a barrier. Some areas should be strictly off-limits. If you're using machinery that could cause her harm (or you, should she distract you), working with paints or chemicals, or even playing with children with small toys that your pet could swallow, it's important that she be kept at a distance.

Baby gates are very useful for restricting your dog's access to certain areas. Make sure the gate is high enough to deter a dog that fancies herself as a high jumper. A gate doesn't shut her out completely—she can still see you without gaining access. Other times, it may be best to crate your dog to keep her safe.

Whisk it into the wash. Run your dog's rug, blanket, or bed-padding through a hot wash at least every other week. "If your dog spends a lot of time outdoors, especially in wooded areas, wash bedding at least once a week," says Dr. Crimi. Regularly laundering bedding helps reduce flea problems and has an unexpected payoff: It can reduce housework by keeping your pooch a lot cleaner and a little less hairy.

Sweep it away. Loose, shed hair attracts irritating dust mites and fleas. Sweeping or vacuuming your dog's shed hair regularly will help keep her healthy.

Give her toys that are dog-safe. When you're buying toys for your dog, or letting her play with toys your children have, you need to take account of her size. Small balls and building blocks can become lodged in a dog's throat. Provide your dog with toys designed for dogs. See page 143 for a selection of dog-safe toys. Socks or a ball of rags are not suitable play material and may cause choking.

Watch out for water. Dogs are often tempted to solve a drought in their water bowl by turning to an open toilet. Misjudging their balance and the depth of the bowl, though, can place them at risk of drowning if they're small enough. Also, there may be harmful bacteria in the water, which could make your dog sick and toilet disinfectants could cause poisoning. Close toilet seats—and keep your dog's water bowls full.

Grow pet-friendly plants. Your dog may occasionally fancy licking a plant or testing her tastebuds on a flower. Mistletoe and poinsettias are common plants that can cause vomiting and diarrhea in dogs, but your pet is unlikely to eat enough of them to do herself harm.

Oleander, dumbcane, and sago palm, though, are plants that can cause serious poisoning even if only a small amount is consumed. In the case of sago palm, the nuts that the plant produces can cause liver damage. Take care to keep your dog on a leash if you're out walking in places where these plants grow.

Take care with lawn care. Treating your lawn for ants, slugs, and other destructive pests is often necessary. But remember that these chemicals taste just as good to your dog as they do to pests.

Kennel your dog or house her elsewhere when you're using these products. As with household cleaning substances, store these chemicals high, and, when you're using them, don't turn your back even for a moment.

Keep the yard dog-friendly. Provide shaded areas in the yard where your dog can get shelter from hot sun. Also make sure there is plenty of cool water for your dog to drink. When winter comes, make sure that your dog can shelter from the cold, wind, rain, and snow.

Clean up your dog's stools in the yard on a regular basis because they attract flies and may contain parasites.

Give her maximum security. Fence the yard securely, or provide a safe run. Car accidents are still among the most common causes of dog injuries. Always check the gate on your fence to make sure it's locked securely before letting your dog outside for her afternoon sun session. If your pooch is a digger, take a regular walk around the yard to make sure she hasn't dug herself an escape route. If you choose a run instead of a fence, make sure the area is safe and she can't inch her way into danger.

Fence around in-ground pools. Many dogs love to swim but even the best canine swimmers can drown in a backyard pool. Keep the pool fenced, and supervise your dog whenever she has a dip.

PART TWO

QUICK RELIEF FROM COMMON COMPLAINTS

Every dog gets sick now and then. Usually all that's needed is a little straightforward, on-the-spot treatment, with some ongoing care. It's a wonderful feeling to know you have the knowledge and skills to give your dog relief just when he needs it most.

Allergies

Dogs don't get runny eyes or sneezing fits when ragweed's in full bloom, but they do suffer from many of the same allergies that humans have to put up with—and then some. "Besides fleas, the most common culprits for a dog's allergies are dust mites, various pollens, molds, wool, and feathers," says James Noxon, D.V.M., staff dermatologist at the Veterinary Teaching College of Iowa State University in Ames. Tobacco smoke and perfumes can also cause allergies in some dogs.

While humans with allergies often sneeze and wheeze, dogs usually itch—badly. In some cases they'll scratch their skin raw as they try to make the itching go away. They'll also spend a lot of time licking their feet or rubbing their faces, says Dr. Noxon.

Itching is not always caused by allergies, adds Dr. Noxon. In fact, there are dozens of problems, from skin infections to internal illnesses, that can kick scratching into high gear. So it's worth calling your vet to find out what's going on. When allergies are to blame—and that's more often than not—there's a lot you can do to stop the itching and soothe the skin. Here's what veterinarians advise.

While humans with allergies tend to sneeze and wheeze, dogs like this Irish wolfhound pup respond to allergies with a good scratch.

Stop itching with a cake pan. Dogs with allergies often act as though their feet are lollipops, licking and biting them for hours at a time. This is probably because the feet pick up a lot of pollen and dust, says Laurel Kaddatz, D.V.M., a veterinarian in private practice in Fairport, New York. One way to give quick relief is to put some water in a cake pan or a small bucket and keep it by the front or back door. This way you can give her feet a quick rinsing whenever she comes inside. Just be sure to dry her feet, especially between the toes. Otherwise the skin will get irritated and itch even more.

Wash away the itch. No matter what's making your dog itch, giving her a cool soak will often provide soothing—if temporary—relief. "When the skin is dry, itching will be worse," explains Dr. Kaddatz. "So you want to keep your dog's skin clean and moist." Cool water by itself may stop the scratching, he adds. To make the bath even more effective, add a little colloidal oatmeal (such as Aveeno) to the bath water. This is very soothing for itchy skin. "While this will provide relief only for about 24 to 48 hours, it will get your dog through the worst times," says Dr. Noxon.

This terrier-mix is having a cool bath to quickly ease his itching. A moisturizing shampoo is being used to give additional comfort.

Keep skin supple. When you bathe your dog, use a moisturizing shampoo, suggests Eileen Gabriel, a professional dog groomer in Yorktown Heights, New York. "Keeping her skin supple will help keep your dog from itching and scratching," she explains.

Slip on some socks. To protect your dog from self-inflicted scratching wounds, try covering her back feet with a pair of toddler's socks. They will help to soften the damage from her nails. Likewise, some vets recommend slipping a baby's stretchy pajama over your dog if she is hurting

Some of the small terriers, such as this Scottish terrier, seem especially subject to allergic skin reactions.

herself by scratching. Then, even if your dog does scratch, the fabric from the pajama will give her skin some protection.

Protect skin from the inside out. One of the best ways to ease itchy skin is to give your dog supplements containing essential fatty acids, such as omega-3s or omega-6s. Available from vets and pet supply stores, they are safe and very effective, although they don't work quickly—it may take from two to four weeks before you see results. Follow the instructions on the label. And if your dog doesn't like swallowing a pill, dip it in a little peanut butter first.

Roll up your sleeves. It's no one's idea of a good time, but sweeping and vacuuming the house more often is one of the best ways to stop allergies. Even though you can't see them, every room in your house has millions of allergy-causing dust mites, microscopic creatures that live in mattresses, on drapes, and under the beds. You can't get rid of them entirely, but regular house cleaning will help reduce their numbers to tolerable levels, says William H. Miller, Jr., V.M.D., professor of dermatology at Cornell University's College of Veterinary Medicine in Ithaca, New York. At least once a week you should vacuum drapes, carpets, and upholstery

BREED SPECIFIC

Any dog can get allergies, but they seem to be most common in Labrador and golden retrievers, as well as in some of the smaller terriers, such as Scottish and West Highland white terriers.

throughout the house, paying special attention to the areas where your dog sleeps, says Dr. Noxon.

It's also a good idea to wash pillow cases, throw rugs, and bedding in hot water once a week. This will kill the mites before they settle in again, explains Dr. Noxon.

While you're cleaning, take a few minutes to change the filters in furnaces, air conditioners, or air humidifiers. This will help reduce the amount of dust—and dust mites— that can trigger allergy flare-ups in your dog.

This Labrador retriever puppy sleeps peacefully on a polished floor, which is less likely to harbor dust mites than carpet.

Since mold is a common cause of allergies, you'll also want to clean areas where mold collects, such as in the bathroom, in refrigerator drip pans, and in air-conditioner grilles, advises Dr. Miller. "The closer your dog gets to allergens, the more reactions she'll have. So do not let your dog nose around in a damp moldy basement," he says.

"In some regions of the country where the humidity levels run high, there is no escaping molds," adds Dr. Noxon. "But you can use a dehumidifier to lessen the problem of molds." Just be sure to clean out the dehumidifier pan at least once a week with a bleach solution to discourage any molds that may have collected there, he adds. Otherwise, the molds will grow in the dehumidifier pan as well.

Give her a new hangout. If nothing else seems to help, you may want to consider keeping your dog in the kitchen or another uncarpeted room, at least while she sleeps, suggests Dr. Miller. "Dogs are most likely to be exposed to dust mites when they join the rest of the family in the living areas of the house, such as bedrooms and the living room," he explains.

Farewell the feathers. The feathers and down in many pillows are a perfect breeding ground for dust mites. But mites don't consider a synthetic pillow the same cozy home-sweet-home. Buy a synthetic pillow for your dog to sleep on, says Dr. Miller, and see if this helps reduce her itching.

Keep her indoors. Dogs that are allergic to pollen usually suffer worst in the early morning and again in the evening, when pollen counts are highest. One way to reduce her exposure to pollen is to keep her indoors during these times in the spring and summer months.

FAST FIX The quickest way to soothe your dog's itchy feet is to put a few inches of cool water in the tub, add Epsom salts according to the directions on the package, and let her stand in the water for five to 10 minutes. Don't let her drink the water because it will have a mild laxative effect.

Head for the medicine chest. Many over-the-counter antihistamines, including Benadryl and Tavist, can be used for dogs. They do the trick for between 25 and 40 percent of dogs suffering from allergies, says Dr. Noxon. Because the dose depends on the body weight of your dog, you will need to ask your veterinarian how much to give her.

WHEN FOOD BITES BACK

Does your dog gobble her kibble only to pay for it later? Is she scratching so much that the fur is literally flying? Although allergies are usually caused by fleas, pollen, or other environmental things, they can also be caused by what you put in the food bowl.

Food allergies are not as common as other forms of allergies in dogs, but they can be equally frustrating, says James Noxon, D.V.M., staff dermatologist at the Veterinary Teaching College of Iowa State University in Ames. They can be tricky to recognize because a dog may develop allergies even when she's been eating the same food all her life. "The problem is not due to a change in food so much as a change in the body's reaction to the food," he explains. Changing brands usually doesn't help because most commercial dog foods contain similar ingredients, such as corn, dried skim milk, or whey.

To find out if your dog has food allergies, put her on an elimination diet, in which you give her a food, available from veterinarians, that contains ingredients with a protein source she's never had before, such as venison, turkey, lamb, or duck. You'll need to stop giving her snacks and even chewable medicines, as well. If she really does have food allergies, the itching will usually subside within about 12 weeks.

The next step is to find out exactly what ingredients were causing the problems. This is done by slowly reintroducing various ingredients, one at a time, until you discover one that sets off the itching again. (Your vet will provide you with the "test" foods.) Once that happens, the rest is easy. All you'll have to do is buy foods and snacks that contain none of the offending ingredient or ingredients, says Dr. Noxon.

There isn't a cure for food allergies, which can escalate to severe diarrhea or bad skin reactions. So you'll have to monitor her diet closely to make sure unauthorized foods don't slip in and start the problems again.

This German shepherd-mix no longer eats wheat, which has cleared up her allergies. Now she only has the occasional itch.

Anal Sac Troubles

Just as humans shake hands when they meet, dogs sniff each other's bottoms. Every dog has a unique scent, and sniffing is their way of saying, "Hello! Who are you?"

Your dog's scent originates in the anal sacs—two storage areas on either side of the anus that contain an odoriferous fluid. When dogs have a bowel movement, some of the fluid is released. This allows them to mark their territory and introduce themselves to other dogs. It also lets them know who else has been paying a visit to their neighborhood.

The sacs normally empty without trouble. But sometimes the fluid backs up—and the sacs become impacted. The main reason for this, particularly in smaller dogs, is that the openings leading from the sacs are too small for the fluid to drain easily. Sometimes, the stools aren't firm enough to exert the necessary pressure on the sacs, or the fluid inside the sacs becomes too thick to get out. Regardless of the cause, the accumulating fluid causes the sacs to swell and become inflamed, making them itchy and uncomfortable. Blocked anal sacs can also get infected, says Laurel Kaddatz, D.V.M., a veterinarian in private practice in Fairport, New York.

Dogs with blocked anal sacs often get temporary relief by licking the area. They'll also try to ease their discomfort by scooting across the floor, giving their bottoms a little scratch. The problem with scooting is that it can irritate the area even more, says James Noxon, D.V.M., a staff dermatologist at the Veterinary Teaching College of Iowa State University in Ames.

Giving Relief

Blocked anal sacs certainly aren't pleasant, but they're rarely serious. And most of the time, they're easy to treat: Removing the fluid from the sacs—a procedure called "expressing"—will relieve the uncomfortable pressure. Most folks take their dogs to the vet to have it done. But it's not difficult to do at home. Here's how.

• Expressing the anal sacs takes a little bit of time, so you need to find a comfortable place to work. For small dogs, the easiest thing is to put them on a table covered with newspaper, says John Giannone, D.V.M., a veterinarian in private practice in Yorktown Heights, New York.

CALL FOR HELP

Dogs are not happy to have their bottoms bothered, but you can usually empty the anal sacs without getting too many complaints. If the area seems unusually tender, or your dog continues to scoot or lick the anal area, you'll need to call your vet.

Don't waste any time if you notice swelling, growths, or sores in the anal area. These may be signs of an anal sac infection, abscesses, polyps, or a type of cancer called anal sac adenocarcinoma, which can cause some of the same symptoms as blocked anal sacs—and is a lot more serious.

The anal sacs are easy to reach for treatment. They're located on either side of the anus, at the four and eight o'clock positions.

Holding the tail out of the way, gently press the skin next to the sacs and squeeze carefully. Don't forget to wear gloves, and use a tissue or piece of gauze to catch the fluid.

You can put larger dogs in a tub or the shower, where the mess can be easily cleaned and the dog sponged off afterward. Otherwise, newspapers spread on the floor will work fine.

• To keep your hands clean, it's a good idea to wear a pair of disposable gloves, says Dr. Giannone. Lubricate the fingers of the gloves with petroleum or K-Y jelly. You'll also want to be holding a tissue or wad of cotton to catch the fluid that will come out of the sacs, he says.

• Recruit someone to gently restrain your dog, with one arm around his neck and the other around his abdomen. Dogs don't enjoy having their bottoms tampered with, and you're going to need some help holding him still.

• The anal sacs are located at the four and eight o'clock positions around the anus. Press the skin with your fingers behind the sac and gently "milk" it. In most cases, the secretions inside will come right out. "You can express one sac at a time or you can do both together," says Dr. Giannone. Just be sure to use a light touch, he warns. Pressing too hard can damage the sac, causing bleeding or other serious problems.

Preventing Problems

Lots of dogs will have anal sac trouble at least once in their lives, and for some it can be an ongoing problem. Even though it's rarely serious, dogs do get uncomfortable—and the condition is not a lot of fun to treat. To prevent the sacs from getting blocked in the future, here's what veterinarians advise.

Scrap the table scraps. It's hard to say no when your canine disposal unit is nosing around the dinner table for a handout, but giving dogs table scraps can cause soft stools, which aren't firm enough to help the anal sacs empty naturally, says Dr. Giannone.

Clear the way. For long-haired dogs especially, stools can get trapped in the hair around the anus. This can irritate the anal area, leading to blocked anal sacs later on. Trimming the hair around your dog's bottom will keep the area cleaner, so he's less likely to have problems.

Bad Breath

A pooch's breath may never be kissably sweet, but it shouldn't be staggeringly bad, either. Most of the time, bad breath is caused by the remains of your pet's last meal, says Gregg DuPont, D.V.M., a veterinarian in private practice in Seattle. The longer food particles stay in her mouth, the ranker her breath is likely to be.

In addition, bad breath is sometimes caused by such things as an upset stomach, tooth decay, or a build-up of plaque—a sticky, bacteria-laden substance that often accumulates on the teeth.

The following tips will help to keep your dog's breath clean and fresh.

Brush often. The best way to beat your dog's bad breath is to brush her teeth, says Robert Wiggs, D.V.M., a veterinarian in private practice in Dallas. If she's not used to brushing,

CALL FOR HELP

If you've been brushing your dog's teeth regularly for a week or two and her breath still smells like last week's garbage, she could have a serious problem—an abscessed tooth, for example. Paradoxically, overly sweet breath is also a problem because it can be a sign of diabetes. An ammonia odor, on the other hand, can be caused by kidney disease. In fact, any change in her usual doggy breath should probably be checked out by your vet.

A quick way to improve your dog's breath is to wipe the outside of the teeth with a cloth, or a "finger brush," available from pet supply stores.

start out by putting a little beef broth, garlic water, or canned meat on your finger or a washcloth and rub the outer surfaces of the teeth.

Once she's used to having her mouth handled, you can graduate to a toothbrush made especially for dogs, says Dr. Wiggs. "Don't be alarmed by a little blood on the bristles the first few times you brush," he says. "This is normal since a dog's gums are not used to being brushed," he explains.

Add a little paste. The best way to freshen your dog's breath is to brush her teeth with a toothpaste specially formulated for dogs, says Dr. Wiggs. Don't use human toothpastes because they contain detergents and other chemicals, which, when swallowed, will upset your dog's stomach. "You can teach a dog to do a lot of things, but I've never seen one trained to rinse and spit," he adds.

Offering crunchy snacks such as carrots and apples will not only help your dog keep her teeth clean, but will also keep her breath fresh.

FAST FIX When you don't have time for real brushing, try wiping the outside of your dog's teeth, where 85 percent of smelly plaque occurs, with a cotton washcloth or gauze—even a quick swipe over will make a difference.

Play fetch and floss. Dogs love to chew, and some chew toys have the added advantage of keeping the teeth clean. Dr. Wiggs recommends giving your dog a rope-like chew toy, such as the Booda Bone. The strands of rope will act like dental floss every time your dog chews. Just be sure the frayed end of the toy isn't tangled or knotted, and don't play tug-of-war with it, says Dr. Wiggs. "It could catch in your dog's teeth and possibly pull one out."

Quell it with crunchy snacks. Dogs rarely refuse a snack, and crunchy foods act like little brushes in the mouth, scouring the teeth and helping to keep the breath pleasant. "Carrots are good for cleaning teeth and for freshening breath," says Dr. DuPont. Apples are also good, as are hard, biscuit-type snacks.

Give her a special food. A pet food manufacturer has developed a dry food called Science Diet T/D, which is specifically designed to clean your dog's teeth by removing the plaque as she chews. It has a fibrous texture and doesn't shatter the way regular kibble does. When your dog takes a bite, her teeth will sink into the food, causing a scraping action that cleans the teeth.

Hold the sticky stuff. It's always a good idea to avoid soft, sticky snacks, like liver treats or peanut butter. They can stick to the teeth for hours, with predictable results, says Dr. DuPont.

Skip the sprays. Save your money when it comes to chlorophyll tablets or other temporary breath fresheners, says Dr. DuPont. "Masking a dog's bad breath with sprays or tablets is fighting a losing battle. Instead, get to the source of the trouble by daily brushing her teeth."

POOCH PUZZLER

What gives puppies "puppy breath"?

When puppies come to you, tails and tongues a-wagging, you'll probably catch a whiff of "puppy breath." The smell is a mixture of sweet and sour, and there's no mistaking it. All puppies have this distinctive smell, no matter what their size or breed. "It has to do with the bacteria levels in puppies' mouths," says Gregg DuPont, D.V.M., a veterinarian in private practice in Seattle. When puppies are teething, the gums bleed slightly, and this provides a perfect environment for bacteria to thrive. It is these large populations of bacteria that produce the sweet smell in their breath.

As puppies mature into dogs, the bacteria levels decline, and so does the puppy smell.

Bleeding

Dogs' full-steam-ahead approach to life is one of their most appealing qualities. But there are times when this exuberance gets them into trouble, and they plow full-steam-ahead onto broken glass or into barbed wire, cutting themselves in the process. Most cuts and scrapes aren't so bad. They just need a calm owner and a little first aid to clean them and bandage them up. With deeper cuts, bleeding can be harder to stop. For deep puncture wounds, a bad cut, or a bite, a vet's help may be needed.

No matter how minor the wound and how sweet your dog is normally, pain can make her do things she doesn't mean—like snap at you while you're tending her wounds. It's a good idea to muzzle an injured dog before performing first aid, says Dennis Jensen, D.V.M., a veterinarian in private practice in Houston. See page 9 for information on how to muzzle your dog.

Whether wounds are slight or serious, there's a lot you can do to control bleeding and help wounds heal more quickly.

Everyday Nicks and Cuts

Shallow cuts are a nuisance rather than anything serious. It's quite easy to stop the bleeding by pressing firmly on the wound for a few minutes with a clean piece of cloth. Once the bleeding's under control, there are a few things you need to do to speed healing and prevent infections from getting started.

Clean the area. Wash the wounded area thoroughly to clean away bacteria and prevent infection. Soap and water will do, but it's best to use a mild antiseptic solution that contains chlorhexidine, available from drugstores.

Give her a trim. Once the bleeding has stopped and the wound is clean, it's important to keep it clean. With long-haired dogs in particular, you may want to trim hair away from the wound to prevent it from getting into the cut as it heals, says Dr. Jensen.

After trimming the hair, apply some K-Y jelly to the wound. This will stick to all the hair that fell down, says Stuart Gluckman, D.V.M., a veterinarian in private practice in Mendon, New York. "Remove the jelly with a tissue and all the cut fur will come with it."

Deep Cuts

Serious cuts—from running through a sliding glass door, for example, or stepping on a jagged piece of metal—don't happen often, but when they do you need to be prepared and act quickly. Your first priority will be to stem the flow of blood. Here's what you need to do.

Put it under pressure. The best way to stop bleeding is to apply direct pressure to the wound, says Dr. Gluckman. Use a clean towel, handkerchief, or cloth, or even your hand in a pinch. The bleeding should slow within a few minutes. If the towel is quickly saturated with blood, apply another one over the top. Don't remove the first one because you may break

Stop the bleeding by applying pressure directly to the wound. Keep pressing firmly until the bleeding stops.

the blood clot that's forming over the wound. Keep pressing until the bleeding stops.

If bleeding doesn't ease in a few minutes, you may need to apply pressure to one of your dog's pressure points—places where arteries are fairly near the surface of the skin. Pressing on a pressure point compresses the artery, inhibiting the blood flow to the wounded area. Serious bleeding is potentially life-threatening, so deal with it immediately and head straight for the veterinarian. The major pressure points you should know about are:

• Upper inside of the front legs. Pressure here helps control bleeding from the lower front legs.

• Upper inside of the rear legs. Pressure here helps control bleeding from the lower hind legs.

• Underside of the tail. Pressure here helps control bleeding from the tail.

Spare the tourniquet. Tightly tied tourniquets make good movie drama when Benji is down for the count. But in real life, tourniquets can do more damage than good, says Dr. Gluckman. "Use tourniquets only as a last resort to save a dog from bleeding to death," he says. "I've seen too many cases of tissue death from tourniquets that have been applied incorrectly or too tightly."

Give her a lift. Carry your dog as much as possible if she is bleeding heavily, until you reach a veterinary clinic, says Dr. Gluckman. "If she continues to walk, she'll bleed more with each heartbeat."

Paw Pad Problems

Most cuts occur on the pads of the paws. While these are rarely serious, they can be a problem because they may reopen when your dog walks around, says Dr. Jensen. You can't get your dog to put her feet up until her paw is

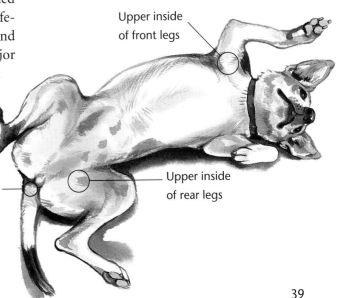

Upper inside of front legs

Upper inside of rear legs

Underside of tail

healed, but there are ways to keep the wound closed and healthy, and free from infection.

Clean it well. Cuts on the paw pads can get dirty in a hurry, so it's important to clean them well, preferably with a little antiseptic soap (such as Betadine scrub) recommends John Giannone, D.V.M., a veterinarian in private practice in Yorktown Heights, New York.

Protect it from the elements. Although wounds often heal faster when they're open to the air, paw pad cuts need to be bandaged to prevent infection as well as additional bleeding, says Dr. Giannone. Once you've cleaned the paw, pat it dry gently. Then put a little antibiotic ointment on a gauze pad and place it over the wound. Wrap some gauze around the foot, going up to the wrist. (Don't wrap the toes because you need to watch for swelling.) Use thick gauze—at least one-quarter to one-

Bandage the foot and wrist firmly, but not too tightly, leaving the toes free so that you can check for swelling.

CALL FOR HELP

Most cuts look a lot more serious than they really are. Bite wounds, on the other hand, usually don't look so bad and may not be bleeding at all. But looks can be deceiving. Bites often leave deep puncture wounds with narrow openings, which means that bacteria from saliva can be trapped inside. "These bite wounds can get infected very easily," says Stuart Gluckman, D.V.M., a veterinarian in private practice in Mendon, New York. "They're best treated with oral or injected antibiotics prescribed by a veterinarian."

In addition, call your vet if your dog has a cut over an inch long, or if the cut is near the eye or on any other sensitive part of her body.

half inch thick—on foot injuries, says Dr. Jensen. Wrap the gauze with first-aid tape, and change the bandage every 24 hours—sooner if it gets wet or starts to smell bad.

Check your dog's paw periodically to make sure her circulation is not inhibited by the bandage. "If you've wrapped it too tight, you'll notice swelling above the bandage or around the toe area within 24 hours," says Dr. Jensen. If that happens, undo it, clean the paw, and rewrap it—a little bit looser this time.

Cover the bandage. To protect the bandage from dirt and moisture, put a plastic bag around your dog's paw or pop a sock on her whenever she goes outside, says Dr. Gluckman. "Remove it when she comes back in or it's likely to become soaked with her sweat."

Constipation

It's not the most exciting part of owning a dog, but occasionally every owner finds himself standing impatiently at one end of the leash while his dog strains to do his business at the other end.

Thankfully, dogs don't get constipated very often. But every dog may occasionally get blocked up, and no matter how much they strain they can't seem to finish what they started, says Rance Sellon, D.V.M., assistant professor in the Department of Veterinary Clinical Sciences at Washington State University in Pullman.

It's not always easy to tell when dogs are constipated, adds Dennis Jensen, D.V.M., a veterinarian in private practice in Houston. In fact, dogs that are straining often have diarrhea. The only way to tell the difference is to take a close look. Diarrhea will be obvious, of course. With constipation, your dog will have little to show for his efforts.

Constipation can make your dog very uncomfortable until it passes. Here are a few ways you can help.

Pass the pumpkin. High-fiber foods are a great way to stop constipation because dietary fiber enlarges stools, which helps them pass more quickly through the body. Canned pumpkin is a super fiber food that vets recommend and dogs love. Mix some with your pet's food until he's regular again.

Beat it with beans. Dried beans are one of the highest-fiber foods and they make a great addition to your dog's meals. Because they take forever to cook, Dr. Jensen suggests canned beans. "Dogs love canned green beans, which are also high in fiber," he says.

Hand over a little treat. Veterinarians usually advise not giving table scraps to dogs because they can make the stools too soft. But when your dog has constipation, a little softening may be just what he needs. So indulge him with raw or cooked vegetables. But avoid dairy and other high-fat foods, which may give him diarrhea, says Dr. Jensen.

Mix in Metamucil. Another way to keep your pet regular is to mix some Metamucil in with his food. This over-the-counter product is made from psyllium seed husks—a potent natural laxative. Dr. Jensen suggests giving half a teaspoon to small dogs and two teaspoons to larger dogs. Avoid giving Metamucil to dogs with a history of colitis or other bowel conditions because it may cause problems.

Keep up the exercise. Like any other muscle in your dog's body, the large intestine works best when he gets plenty of exercise. Taking him for regular walks (vets usually advise 15 to 20 minutes twice a day) will go a long way toward keeping him regular.

Cooked vegetables are great for treating and preventing constipation.

Coughing

Most dogs will let loose with the occasional "eck" now and then—when they're hacking up some fur or trying to get a piece of grass out of their throats—but they hardly ever cough. When they do start hacking and coughing, it's a fair bet they have a condition known as kennel cough.

Kennel cough is an upper respiratory infection that's readily passed from dog to dog, says Jody Sandler, D.V.M., director of veterinary services for Guiding Eyes for the Blind in Yorktown Heights, New York. It's most common in young dogs, although older dogs can get it too. Despite the name, kennel cough rarely occurs in kennels any more because most businesses require dogs to be vaccinated against it before they check in. But because it's highly contagious, dogs have a higher risk of catching it when they've been in close confinement with other dogs.

Kennel cough is rarely serious and usually clears up on its own in seven to 10 days. Until it goes away, it can be very hard on your dog's throat and may make it hard for her to sleep, says Dr. Sandler. To ease the discomfort, here's what veterinarians advise.

Pour an exotic drink. Juice containing an Asian fruit called loquat is very rich in vitamin A, which boosts immunity and strengthens the mucus membranes of the respiratory tract. "The juice of the loquat is remarkably effective in quieting a cough," says Allen Schoen, D.V.M., a veterinarian in private practice in Sherman, Connecticut. If your dog won't lap up fruit juice containing loquat, you can add a little to her food, or put it directly in her mouth with a needleless syringe. "Don't give it to a dog that has diabetes because it's high in sugar," Dr. Schoen adds. You can buy fruit juice containing loquat at health food stores.

Help her through the night. Dogs with kennel cough are often exhausted—not only because of the underlying infection, but because coughing is hard work. Unfortunately, coughing doesn't go away when you turn out the lights. To help your dog get the healing rest she needs, put a humidifier or vaporizer near her bed. This will

CALL FOR HELP

Kennel cough rarely lasts long, but other coughs may be more serious. Coughing may be a symptom of heart disease or even a collapsed windpipe, which is fairly common in small dogs. "You should not treat a cough at home for longer than three days without having your dog checked by a vet," says Stuart Gluckman, D.V.M., a veterinarian in private practice in Mendon, New York.

If your dog is coughing and also having trouble breathing or has lost her appetite, don't wait even three days before calling your vet, he adds. "The cough from heart disease is a lower, quieter cough than kennel cough," explains Dr. Gluckman. "It often starts gradually and may occur first thing in the morning when the lungs are filled with gunk."

help fill her airways with soothing moisture, says Richard J. Rossman, D.V.M., a veterinarian in private practice in Glenview, Illinois. Humidifiers and vaporizers are easily contaminated with mold, Dr. Rossman adds, so clean the water basins often. "To be safe, use two basins," he suggests. "Let one have a 24-hour dry-out period every other day."

Give her some down time. Kennel cough may not dampen your dog's enthusiasm for fun, but running around will often trigger more coughing, says Stuart Gluckman, D.V.M., a veterinarian in private practice in Mendon, New York. "A burst of activity will increase the airflow through her windpipe and start her coughing," he explains. Until your dog recovers, don't let her get too excited and keep play time to a minimum. Gentle walks are fine, but keep in mind that her throat will be sore and sensitive. Rather than using a collar, use a harness around her chest. And be sure to keep her away from other dogs, or she could pass the infection on to them.

Move ashtrays outside. Cigarette smoke—along with chemical fumes like ammonia—can be very irritating when your dog has kennel cough. To protect her throat and help her heal more quickly, keep the air she breathes clean. If you smoke, do it outside until she recovers. And on cleaning days, put her outside until fumes from polishes and cleaners leave the air.

Give some over-the-counter relief. A quick way to ease coughing is with human cough medicines such as Robitussin, Triaminic, or Vicks-44, says Dr. Gluckman. He recommends giving the full human dose every six

Cough medicines made for humans can help to relieve your dog's cough. Use a needleless syringe to administer the medicine into the side of her mouth.

hours to large dogs 60 pounds or over. A 30-to-40 pound dog can take half the human dose, and smaller dogs can take a quarter of the human dose. Each dog needs a different dose, he adds, so check with your veterinarian for the correct amount.

When giving cough medicines, be sure to read the label carefully, he adds. Avoid cough medicines that contain acetaminophen, which can be dangerous for dogs.

Give some prevention. Vaccines won't help your dog if she already has kennel cough, but they're a great way to prevent it. Available as nasal drops, the vaccines usually target *Bordetella bronchiseptica*, the bacterium that often causes kennel cough. Vaccines are especially helpful when your dog is spending a lot of time with other dogs or will be boarded in a kennel.

"While these kennel cough vaccines are not 100 percent effective, even if your dog does get sick it will be a milder case," says Dr. Sandler. It's a good idea to give the vaccine seven to 14 days before taking your dog to a kennel if he hasn't received it within the previous six months.

Dental Problems

Dogs don't care if they have crooked teeth, so you will never have to buy braces for your basset. They rarely get cavities, either. But dogs, like people, do require regular home dental care. It's the only way to prevent gingivitis and periodontal disease, conditions in which bacteria in the mouth may lead to painful infections or even tooth loss.

"Gingivitis is completely reversible by home oral care," explains Gene Rivers, D.V.M., a veterinarian in private practice in Seattle. "With regular cleaning you can help your dog have a completely healthy mouth."

Most vets recommend brushing your dog's teeth at least twice a week, although every day is better, says Gregg DuPont, D.V.M., a veterinarian in private practice in Seattle. Frequent

This dachshund is having the outer surfaces of his teeth and the gum line brushed with gentle, circular motions.

brushing is especially important if your dog is pregnant or lactating, when hormonal changes make the teeth more vulnerable to bacteria.

Ideally, you should get into the habit of regularly brushing your dog's teeth when he is a puppy and eager to try new things. Older dogs are a bit more reluctant to put up with having their teeth brushed, but there are ways to coax them to open wide, says Dr. DuPont.

Pick your paste. Dog toothpastes come in plenty of tasty flavors, including poultry and beef. Brushing his teeth will be a lot easier if you find a taste he enjoys. If toothpastes don't tempt his tastebuds, try chicken or beef broth, garlic water or even baby food. They are not as effective as toothpaste, but still do the job, says Dr. DuPont. Don't use human toothpaste because it usually contains detergents, and if your dog swallows some, it can cause a stomach upset.

Give him a taste. If your dog isn't used to having his teeth brushed, don't dive right in with a toothbrush, cautions Dr. DuPont. "Start by giving him a taste of dog toothpaste, baby food, or whatever you intend to use," he says. If you do this every day for a week, he'll start looking forward to the treats, which will make brushing his teeth easier later on. Once your dog is eagerly anticipating the new tastes, put some of the toothpaste on a soft-bristled dog toothbrush and let him lick it off. Soon he'll come running for his daily brushing, says Dr. DuPont.

Start slowly. Gradually start to brush the outside of your dog's teeth. "Don't worry too much about brushing the inside of the teeth,"

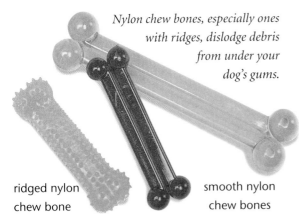

Nylon chew bones, especially ones with ridges, dislodge debris from under your dog's gums.

ridged nylon chew bone

smooth nylon chew bones

says Dr. DuPont. "Your dog's mouth is quite good at self-cleaning this area." Brush the teeth with a gentle, circular motion. Pay special attention to where the gum and teeth meet.

Brush according to breed. "As a general rule, the smaller the dog, the closer attention you must pay to his teeth," says Robert Wiggs, D.V.M., a veterinarian in private practice in Dallas. A smaller mouth means less jawbone for the roots of the teeth. The roots are therefore more shallow, and the teeth are less secure or stable. In these cases, a little disease can quickly lead to tooth loss. Brush your dog's teeth more often and you will help prevent this.

Be prepared to back off. Some dogs hate having their teeth brushed and may bite if you try to force the issue, says Dr. Wiggs. "Some dogs are very mouth shy, and you don't want anyone to get hurt," he says.

Try a compromise. If your dog is truly tightlipped when it comes to having his teeth brushed, take a washcloth or gauze and quickly wipe the outside of his teeth after a meal, says Dr. DuPont. To make this quick-swiping technique even more effective, Dr. Rivers suggests using CHX Gel, available in pet supply stores, which contains an antibacterial ingredient that will help kill germs in the mouth. You could also try a "finger brush" specially made for cleaning the outside of dogs' teeth.

Put his teeth to work. Brushing is an excellent way to keep his teeth clean, but there's also an easier way: give him hard biscuits, which scrub the surfaces of the teeth when he chews.

Give him dry food. Feeding your dog dry food is good for his teeth. Dry kibble doesn't stick to the teeth like canned food, which means it provides less fodder for bacteria. And because it's crunchy, it helps scrub the teeth clean—although it's no substitute for regular brushing.

CALL FOR HELP

Dogs will chomp down on small stones or hard sticks as readily as on a liver treat. If they really bite down hard enough, they may loosen or even break their teeth.

Loose teeth can also be the result of an underlying problem, like an abscess or periodontal disease, says Gregg DuPont, D.V.M., a veterinarian in private practice in Seattle. "Feed your dog a soft diet until you can get him to a vet," says Dr. DuPont. "Don't try to remove a dangling tooth, which can be excruciatingly painful."

"Your dog's teeth can break fairly easily," adds Robert Wiggs, D.V.M., a veterinarian in private practice in Dallas. Ice cubes, a common summertime treat, are often to blame, he says. Opt for ice chips instead.

Diarrhea

There's an unwritten law of nature that says if your dog is going to have diarrhea, it's going to happen on the carpet. The odds increase if you've recently had your carpet cleaned or company is due to arrive in five minutes.

Go easy on your poor pal. Dogs don't like getting diarrhea any more than people do. Unfortunately, they get it a lot more often. While diarrhea may be caused by intestinal infections, mostly it occurs when dogs eat something they shouldn't—like yesterday's trash.

Cleaning bills aside, diarrhea usually isn't anything to worry about, says Kenneth Harkin, D.V.M., assistant professor in the Department of Clinical Sciences at Kansas State University's College of Veterinary Medicine in Manhattan. "It's the body's way of getting rid of something that is causing it distress," he explains.

When her stomach is troubled, this Border collie needs easy-to-digest food such as cooked white rice. Brown rice should be avoided because it can cause further problems.

Veterinarians usually recommend letting diarrhea run its course for a day. But to help your dog feel much better in the meantime, here's what veterinarians advise.

Hold that food. It's a good idea not to feed your dog for 12 to 24 hours when she has diarrhea, Dr. Harkin says. If you don't put food into her system, you won't have the mess coming out. Plus, a temporary fast gives her insides a chance to recover.

Settle her stomach. Once the diarrhea has slowed a bit, you can start feeding your dog a little bit of cooked white rice. White rice is easy to digest and will help firm up soft stools.

"Try rice with hamburger, low-fat cottage cheese, or low-fat yogurt," Dr. Harkin says. It's important to remove as much grease from the hamburger as possible, so either boil it or grill it and pat off excess fat with a paper kitchen towel, he says. "But remember to wait for at least 12 hours after the onset of the diarrhea before giving rice or any other food."

Give her extra liquids. Dogs with diarrhea can lose tremendous amounts of fluid quickly. You can prevent dehydration by leaving out plenty of fresh, clean water, says Brad Fenwick, D.V.M., of the Department of Clinical Sciences at Kansas State University's College of Veterinary Medicine in Manhattan. Dogs with diarrhea are often feeling miserable and may not be up to drinking. Encourage her to drink more by pouring a little Pedialyte in her bowl. This is a "rehydration" solution available

You can check your dog's gums to see if diarrhea has caused dehydration. If her normally moist gums have become dry and tacky, she's lost precious fluids and you need to encourage her to drink.

CALL FOR HELP

Diarrhea usually goes away on its own without causing problems. In some cases, however, it's a symptom of other, more serious conditions. "If your dog is ill for more than a day or has bloody or profuse diarrhea, get her to a vet," says Kenneth Harkin, D.V.M., assistant professor in the Department of Clinical Sciences at Kansas State University's College of Veterinary Medicine in Manhattan. Before you go, collect some of her stool in a plastic bag. Your vet may want to analyze the stool to find out what's causing the problem.

Since dogs with diarrhea can lose lots of precious fluids, it's important to check for signs of dehydration. A quick test is to gently pull down your dog's eyelid. If it sticks to the eye, she could be dangerously low on fluids and you should see a vet right away.

from pharmacies and some supermarkets. Dogs like the taste and it replaces minerals in the body that the diarrhea took out, says Dr. Harkin.

Keep her balanced. Dogs with diarrhea often lose a lot of vitamins and other essential nutrients. Give her some warm, fortified broth, which is packed with nutrients, says Edmund Dorosz, D.V.M., a veterinarian in private practice in Ft. Macleod, Alberta, Canada. He recommends dissolving a beef or chicken bouillon cube in three cups of hot water. When the water cools, add a half teaspoon of baking soda and toss in a quarter teaspoon of powdered garlic.

Long-Term Protection

Until someone figures out a way to keep dogs out of the trash and away from stagnant, muddy water, they're going to keep getting diarrhea.

You can't prevent it entirely, but there are ways to keep your dog's insides calm. Here are a few things you may want to try.

Maintain a steady diet. People get tired of eating the same food all the time, and they assume their dogs do, too. But most dogs are perfectly content eating the same thing every day—and it's good for their digestive tracts, as well. A sudden switch to a new diet is a common cause of diarrhea, says Dr. Harkin.

If you do decide to change brands, do it slowly, he adds. Over a week or so, gradually begin swapping a little bit of her old food for a little bit of the new. Keep adding more of the new food until you've made a complete switch. "You may still see a soft stool for one to two weeks, but this is self-limiting," says Dr. Harkin.

Be careful what you cook. More and more people are giving up commercial dog foods and replacing them with home-cooked meals. Dogs love people foods, but these foods don't always love them back. Milk, cheese, and other dairy foods are a common cause of diarrhea in dogs, says Dr. Fenwick. "Dogs can be even more lactose intolerant than humans," he explains.

Skip the eggs. Many people slip the occasional raw egg into their dog's food because eggs are said to improve their coats. But what you're really doing is increasing the risk of salmonellosis, a type of food poisoning that can cause diarrhea, says Dr. Fenwick.

Leave the leftovers. Don't give your dog any "refrigerator rejects," says Dr. Fenwick. "If it doesn't look or smell fresh enough to eat yourself, it's no good for your dog, either."

Keep cans refrigerated. If you feed your dog canned food, don't leave open cans on the counter, where diarrhea-causing bacteria can grow, says Dr. Fenwick. "If she doesn't eat all of the can of food in one sitting, cover the remainder securely with plastic wrap, pressing out as much air as possible. Then store the food in the refrigerator."

Avoid garbage gut. Almost every dog embarks on the occasional midnight raid on the trash—and pays the price the next day. You can't change your dog's appetite, but you can lock away temptation. To be on the safe side, keep garbage cans tightly closed and behind locked doors, says Dr. Harkin, including the one in the kitchen, which most dogs can open.

Watch the water. It's a good idea to clean your dog's water dish every day, since bacteria from her mouth may accumulate in the bowl and cause diarrhea. And watch to see where your dog is drinking outside, says Dr. Fenwick. Dogs can get viral or bacterial infections from outside water sources, such as mud puddles and stagnant water trapped in old containers lying about the backyard. "Of special concern is *Giardia*, protozoal organisms that occur frequently in slow-moving springs or where groundwater may collect," he says.

For this Labrador-mix, garbage cans are five-star restaurants. But she won't be happy about the diarrhea that might follow later on. Play it safe and lock the can away.

Drooling

Most dogs drool a bit, and some breeds drool more than others. Even though drooling itself isn't a problem, any *change* in your dog's usual drooling may be a sign that something's wrong. Dogs that have something stuck in their mouths will often drool heavily. So will dogs that have gotten into something that's upsetting their stomachs, such as household poisons.

In most cases, of course, drooling is just a natural dog thing. Whether you're faced with a few drips or a flood, here are a few ways to keep things drier.

Cover him in style. The easiest way to keep your house—and your dog—dry is to catch some of the stream with a smart bandanna, suggests Susan Bonhower, a Newfoundland breeder in Cornwall, Ontario, Canada. The more absorbent the fabric, the better it will work, she adds. Fold the bandanna in half diagonally and tie it around his neck so the triangular part covers his chest.

Wipe him down. When your pet's been roughhousing outdoors and is excited and

At suppertime, this golden retriever starts dripping like a faucet. He can't help it, it just comes naturally.

happy, drooling is inevitable. Giving his mouth and jowls a quick wipe with a small towel will keep him dry for a while.

Put out the placemat. As Pavlov proved, the approach of suppertime has dogs drooling in happy anticipation. To keep the floor dry, you may want to put a placemat under his bowl. A few squares of disposable, absorbent paper towels make an effective mat.

Look for trouble. Whether your dog is generally dry or drippy, a sudden increase in saliva demands attention. "A deluge can suddenly start up because your dog is in pain," says Gene Rivers, D.V.M., a veterinarian in private practice in Seattle. It's not uncommon for dogs to get bits of bone or stick lodged behind their back teeth, which often causes heavy drooling, he explains.

BREED SPECIFIC

Dogs with heavy lips and floppy jowls, such as boxers, bloodhounds, Saint Bernards, mastiffs, and Newfoundlands, drool more than most. The loose skin around their mouths traps saliva that will eventually build up and overflow.

It's usually not hard to spot foreign objects. Open your dog's mouth and take a look around. Check his teeth and gums, the upper part of the mouth, and underneath his tongue, says James Ross, D.V.M., chair of the Department of Clinical Sciences at Tufts University School of Veterinary Medicine in North Grafton, Massachusetts. In most cases you can remove small objects with your fingers or a pair of tweezers, he says.

Your dog won't enjoy having your hand in his mouth, and it can take a lot of strength to keep his mouth open long enough to remove whatever's in there. One way to make things easier is to prop the front of his mouth open with a ball, says Dr. Ross. Just make sure the ball is too large for him to swallow, he adds.

Rinse him out. Dogs investigate the world with their mouths and tongues, and they're

CALL FOR HELP

Shoe polish, antifreeze, weed killers, and the green leaves of certain rhododendrons are just some of the potentially toxic substances you may have around your home.

A sudden burst of excessive drooling, along with breathing trouble or bleeding from the mouth or anus, may mean that your dog has consumed a poisonous substance. Drooling with drowsiness is another symptom. Get him to the vet at once, advises James Ross, D.V.M., chair of the Department of Clinical Sciences at Tufts University School of Veterinary Medicine in North Grafton, Massachusetts. If you know what he's gotten into, take a sample with you to the vet, he adds.

Prop your dog's mouth open with a tennis ball, or similar object, while you search for and remove small foreign objects with your fingers or a pair of tweezers.

not very selective about what they lick or chomp on. When the object of their curiosity is toxic—toads, for example, are a common cause of poisoning—the drooling mechanism may go into overdrive. "The result is a lot of frantic head shaking and excessive amounts of saliva tumbling from your dog's mouth," says Dr. Ross. "This may be his way of attempting to flush out the toxins."

To give nature a helping hand, quickly get as much of the toxic substance out of your dog's mouth as you possibly can. "Rinse his mouth out thoroughly," says Dr. Ross. "I use a garden hose with my dogs, running the stream of water through their mouths." After flushing his mouth for several minutes, get him to the vet as quickly as possible, Dr. Ross adds.

Ear Problems

Cute and charming on the outside, dogs' ears often tell a less appealing story on the inside. Ear problems are among the most common conditions veterinarians treat. The insides of the ears are warm and moist, which makes them a perfect breeding ground for mites and other harmful organisms. In fact, mites cause most of a dog's ear troubles throughout his life, says Daryl B. Leu, D.V.M., a veterinarian with a dermatology referral practice in Portland, Oregon. Young dogs get mites more than older ones, while bacteria and yeast affect all age groups, he explains.

Allergies are another leading cause of itchy ears, adds Dr. Leu. And the ears also act as natural magnets for such things as burrs or grass seeds, which can cause irritation and infections.

Since the ears contain not only the hearing system, but also your dog's balance-control center, even minor problems can be very uncomfortable, says L. R. Daniel, D.V.M., a veterinarian in private practice in Covington, Louisiana. And without treatment, minor ear infections can lead to deafness or serious whole-body infections, he explains.

"Most infections or infestations involve the external part of a dog's ear," says Dr. Daniel. "If the inner ear is infected, you could have real trouble." If you ever notice your dog stumbling or off balance, it could indicate an ear infection that needs attention. He'll probably need antibiotics from your vet.

Fortunately, most ear problems are easy to detect early on. All you have to do is take a quick look—and have a sniff. Healthy ears are pink and fresh-looking, without a noticeable smell. When the ears are looking gritty or inflamed, or there's a foul smell coming from them, you can be pretty sure there's a problem.

Mites

When your dog is working himself into a frenzy of head-shaking and ear-scratching, it's worth taking a look for ear mites. These white, crab-like parasites feed on skin flakes and debris inside your dog's ears, and they produce an itch so intense that some dogs will scratch their ears raw trying to make the itching go away.

Though mites themselves are difficult to see, the reddish-brown crusty discharge they leave behind is clearly visible. Even when you know your dog has mites, however, they're not always easy to get rid of. Over-the-counter medications will kill some mites, but others will go on holiday at the base of the tail or some other choice spot, only to return when the medication has

---

BREED SPECIFIC

Since ear infections thrive in the presence of moisture, oil, and heat, they're most common in floppy-eared dogs like basset hounds, spaniels, and weimaraners. Their big ear flaps act like tents, creating little saunas that bacteria and other organisms love.

worn off. Whichever treatment you choose, plan on keeping after the problem for six to eight weeks, which covers the mites' entire life cycle of four weeks, and allows a bit extra to be on the safe side. You'll also have to make checking for mites a regular part of your dog's home healthcare routine because there will always be a new family ready to move in.

Flush his ears. The first step in getting rid of mites is to flush his ears thoroughly. This will not only send some of the ear mites packing, it will also clean out the gunk they leave behind, making it much more difficult for the remaining ear mites to hide.

Soak a wad of cotton balls or a gauze pad in a solution containing equal parts water and vinegar. Hold the pad over the ear opening, gently squeeze in the cleaning solution, and massage it in, advises Dr. Leu. Then mop up as much of the solution and debris as you can with clean cotton balls—and stand back while your dog shakes out some more. Flush again until there's no sign of the red debris and the solution runs clear. It's a good idea to do follow-up flushes once a week for a few weeks, he adds.

Lather him up. Any insecticidal shampoo, such as an over-the-counter flea shampoo, will effectively kill mites in the fur, says Dr. Daniel. Follow up with another bath several weeks later to kill any newly hatched mites or adults that may have escaped the first go-round, he adds.

Oil the mites. Putting mineral oil in your dog's ears will drown some of the mites and also clean the ears and reduce itching, says Dr. Daniel. He recommends placing five to 10 drops of mineral oil in each ear once a day and massaging it in. Continue this for six to eight weeks.

When administering ear drops, hold the ear flap firmly to prevent your dog from shaking his head, and squeeze the required number of drops into the ear.

Give them a dusting. Sprinkling powder—it doesn't matter if it's flea powder, talc, or baby powder—around your dog's head and ears will clog the breathing holes of the mites, making it more difficult for them to survive. It's a good idea to continue dusting your dog every day until the scratching lets up.

Treat all family pets. Mites are mobile creatures and will readily travel from one pet to another. So it's not enough to treat only the dog with ear mites—you have to treat all your pets, says Dr. Leu. This is especially important if you have cats, since the mites that affect dogs actually come from cats.

FAST FIX To prevent problems, clean his ears after his bath using a cotton ball dipped in a little hydrogen peroxide.

Maintaining your firm grip on the ear flap, massage the base of the ear gently to work the drops into all the nooks and crannies that can harbor the problem.

Ear Infections

In dogs (as in people), ear infections are extremely common. "The ears have the three things needed for bacteria and yeast to thrive: Heat, moisture, and oil," explains Dr. Leu. Dogs that go swimming a lot or live in humid climates have an especially high risk of ear infections, he adds.

Ear infections usually cause the inside of your dog's ear to become red, hot, and swollen, and are quite painful. Infections can also make the ears incredibly smelly—which is why the easiest way to tell if the ears are infected is to take a sniff.

"If your eyes roll back in your head, he's got a yeast or bacterial infection in there," says Dr. Daniel. The smell from bacterial infections

is strong and sour, while yeast infections smell a bit like a wet tennis shoe, adds Dr. Leu. Ear infections that last more than a few days should be seen by a veterinarian. In many cases, though, the infections are not severe and you can take care of them at home. Here's how.

Remove the goop. Before you can clean your dog's ears properly, you will need to remove the gunk that infections leave behind. Gently reach into the ear with a bit of gauze or the corner of a dry, soft washcloth and scoop away as much of the gunk inside the ear as you can, says Dr. Daniel.

It is best to avoid using a cotton swab as it may push debris further into your dog's ears, which may make the infection worse.

Wash them well. Flushing the ears with a solution made from equal parts vinegar, rubbing alcohol, and water will kill infection-causing organisms in the ears. "The vinegar changes the ear's pH level, which means the bacteria or yeast won't be able to survive. The alcohol helps dry the ear so they won't return," explains Dr. Daniel.

He recommends flushing the ears liberally twice a day, using a piece of gauze or a cotton ball to squeeze fluid into the ear opening and using your other hand to massage the base of the ear and distribute the fluid. The alcohol in the solution can sting, he adds. If it stings so much that your dog won't sit still for the treatments, it's fine to leave out the alcohol.

Most ear infections will clear up within a week using home remedies. If your dog's ears still smell bad after that, he probably has a more serious infection and will need prescription medications to clear it up.

Foreign Objects

Dogs shove their heads into all sorts of places, from interesting burrows in the ground to hedges that trap tennis balls. Along the way their ears act like little Hoovers, picking up twigs, burrs, and even small stones. Most objects in the ears fall out as easily as they fell in. But if they work their way into the ear canal, they can be irritating, painful and possibly dangerous, says Dr. Daniel.

"A dog with something inside his ear canal, whether it's a tick or a stick, is going to be real jumpy when you try to get a closer look," says Dr. Daniel. In some instances, you won't even be

This beagle's ears are checked regularly for such things as burrs and grass seeds, which can cause irritation and infection if they work their way inside.

able to see what's causing your dog's distress. What you may notice is your dog scratching and pawing his head—or, in some cases, holding his head down on the side with the problem. In this case, says Dr. Daniel, the object's likely to be too far in the ear for you to remove it anyway, and you should take your dog to your veterinarian. He'll use a specialized ear instrument to take a closer look.

If the object in your dog's ear is clearly visible, you will probably be able to remove it yourself, either with your fingers or a pair of blunt-tipped tweezers, says Dr. Leu. Serrated-edged grippers called hemostats are also good for removing visible, easy accessible objects from your dog's ear, he says. These are available in pet supply stores, as well as most sporting goods or drug stores.

Hold his head. Have someone hold your dog's head very still—and try using your fingers to remove the object. "He's going to jump," says Dr. Daniel, "so go slowly." Pull the object out carefully, without pushing it any farther into the ear. If you can't reach it, don't make things worse by shoving it farther down.

Float it out. Dr. Daniel says flushing the ear with water using a turkey baster or ear bulb will sometimes float an object out. Don't blast the water in there by squeezing the baster's bulb too firmly. Just gently drip water into your dog's ear to try to release the object, he says.

Add some slip. To remove prickly objects like burrs, it's helpful to lubricate them with 10 to 20 drops of mineral oil. Even if the object won't come out, or you can't see the object at all, the mineral oil will help ease your dog's discomfort until you can get him to the vet.

Eye Problems

Eye problems are always scary because vision is such a precious sense. But the eyes are surprisingly sturdy and will usually recover as long as you take care of the problem quickly.

But because dogs don't depend on sight as much as people do, they may have vision problems for years before their owners realize anything is wrong, and the condition is diagnosed. "Dogs are very good at compensating with their other senses," says Ken Abrams, D.V.M., a veterinary ophthalmologist in private practice in Warwick, Rhode Island.

When you know what to look for, however, many eye problems are easy to spot. A red, blood-shot eye, for example, could be a sign of glaucoma, in which pressure inside the eye increases. Another serious eye problem is dry eye, in which the eyes don't have a normal covering of tears. Dogs with dry eye will often have pus on the eyeball, and they need to be treated by a veterinarian right away.

A much more common condition is conjunctivitis, which causes inflam-

mation around the white of the eye and the lining of the eyelids. Conjunctivitis causes sore, swollen, red eyes, and often a discharge. It's frequently caused by allergies or minor irritation, and it usually isn't serious, says Dr. Abrams.

In addition, any small, sharp object can scratch the cornea—the clear, outer portion of the eye. Scratched corneas are very common, says James Ross, D.V.M., chair of the Department of Clinical Sciences at Tufts University School of Veterinary Medicine in North Grafton, Massachusetts. A scratched cornea usually makes dogs intensely sensitive to light, and the eyes will water.

To treat and prevent simple eye problems, here's what veterinarians recommend.

Dogs with very prominent eyes, such as pugs, have a high risk of developing eye problems.

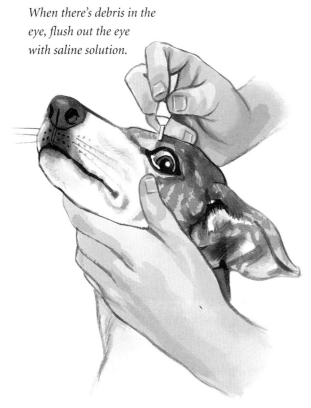

When there's debris in the eye, flush out the eye with saline solution.

If you're using ointment, squeeze a quarter-inch line directly onto the eye. Gently massage the upper and lower eyelids together to spread the ointment completely over the surface of the eye. Then give her a treat for having been such a good patient.

Don't pull it out. When a foreign body is lodged in the cornea and flushing with saline doesn't remove it, get your dog to a veterinarian immediately. "Never attempt to pull out a particle that is protruding from the eye," cautions Dr. Abrams. For as long as you leave it alone, the object will act like a plug. If you remove it the wrong way, you could damage the eye and allow

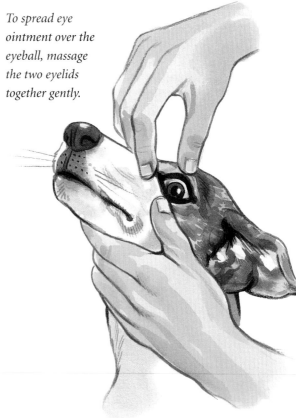

To spread eye ointment over the eyeball, massage the two eyelids together gently.

Flush out the debris. If you can see something in your dog's eye, wash the area with a saline eye solution, says Dr. Abrams. "The kind without preservatives is best since some dogs can be sensitive to these. You can also use artificial tears or an ophthalmologic ointment."

Before you try to put drops or ointment in your dog's eye, enlist a friend's help. "It's always a lot easier if there are two of you to hold and calm her," says Dr. Abrams.

Pick up her chin so her nose points to the ceiling. She'll automatically look down to protect the cornea, says Dr. Abrams. Gently pull the upper eyelid back and squirt a drop of solution on the surface of the eye.

Emma

Imagine living in the world without hearing and with virtually no eyesight. Then imagine you can't communicate in words with those around you. These are the problems that beset Emma, a deaf and nearly blind Australian shepherd. But using her sense of touch, Emma can navigate around a room and memorize its layout almost instantly. If Emma's looking for her owner, Miranda Spindel, of Ft. Collins, Colorado, in an open area, she searches in circles, like the herding dog that she is. When she's close enough, her sense of smell kicks in and she gets excited and makes a beeline for her target.

Like most blind dogs, her sense of smell helps her recognize people as well as other canines, says Spindel. When she's in an unfamiliar place, she slows down and walks at a snail's pace until she is sure of herself and her surroundings.

Spindel has taught Emma basic obedience commands, only instead of words she uses touches. A touch on the rump, for instance, means "sit," while a touch on the chest is "stay." Emma also responds to jiggles of the leash when she's out on a walk, much like a horse responds to reins.

Spindel's biggest challenge is the command "come." She can use a flashing light at night, which Emma's limited vision picks up. But in daytime it's much harder. Spindel has devised a special collar using the parts from a radio-controlled car so that she can command "come" without a leash, using a vibration.

Like people, dogs have the ability to work around their disabilities. Emma is certainly living proof of this. "Most people don't know there is anything different about Emma until I tell them," says Spindel.

harmful bacteria to get in. It's important to continue flushing the eye with saline solution until you can get your dog to the vet.

Clean her eyes. If your dog's eyes have a thick discharge, gently clean them with a soft, damp cloth as often as needed. If there's no improvement within 24 hours, take your dog to your veterinarian, who may need to prescribe antibiotics to clear up an infection.

"If the discharge is watery, it could signal an allergic type of conjunctivitis and in that case the backs of the third eyelids will have to be examined. You'll need to get your veterinarian to do this," Dr. Abrams advises.

Give her eye drops. When your dog's eyes are dry and sore, lubricate them with eye drops such as Opticlear Eyewash, available in pet supply stores and catalogs.

If the dryness still persists, take your dog to your veterinarian who will check if she is suffering from dry-eye syndrome.

Protect her from herself. We all want to rub a sore eye and your dog is no exception. You'll help her injured eye heal if you keep her from scratching at it, says Dr. Ross. An Elizabethan collar should do the trick. This is a cone-shaped plastic collar which can be slipped over her head, protecting her face from her paws. Such collars are available from pet stores, or you can easily make one at home. See page 79 for instructions.

Go for the scissors. Some dogs need a haircut more for the sake of their eyes than for their general appearance. "It's always a good idea to

Dogs like this German shepherd-mix love to ride with the wind in their faces, but the wind can irritate the eyes. Veterinarians advise keeping dogs restrained in the car and keeping windows open only a few inches.

Soothe her with a compress. When your dog's eyes are sore and inflamed, covering them with a warm, damp compress will help to ease her discomfort. Using lukewarm water, wet a clean, soft cloth, wring it out and gently hold it against her eyes for five minutes. If she's upset at having both eyes covered, simply apply the cloth to one eye first, then apply a fresh compress to the other eye.

CALL FOR HELP

For pop-eyed breeds like pugs, shih tzus and Lhasa apsos, an eyeball popping out of its socket is a real possibility—and a real emergency. The eyeball doesn't actually pop all the way out, but gets pushed past the midway point of the bony eye socket. You'll suddenly notice the eye protruding more than is normal.

"Ninety percent of the time this injury occurs in a food-bowl fight," says Ken Abrams, D.V.M., a veterinary ophthalmologist in private practice in Warwick, Rhode Island.

An eye that pushes out of its socket needs immediate treatment. Before and during the trip to the vet, says Dr. Abrams, rinse the eye thoroughly with a saline solution and cover it with a saturated gauze pad, making sure to keep the pad wet.

trim hair away from a dog's face, especially for breeds such as Lhasa apsos, shih tzus and Pekingese," says Dr. Abrams. This keeps hairs from rubbing the surface of the eyes, preventing scratched corneas and infections.

For dogs that were born with that shaggy, overgrown look, like Old English sheepdogs and bearded collies, it's best to leave the hair over their eyes, since it can actually protect them from dust and debris.

Keep her head inside the car. It's a good idea to keep car windows open just a few inches only when your dog is on board. Most dogs love sticking their heads out of the window and feeling the wind in their faces, but this is an open invitation to twigs and debris to fly in to their eyes and do damage.

Flatulence

All dogs get a little gassy at one time or another, and nobody loves them the less for it. But excessive flatulence can test the patience of even the most devoted owner.

Flatulence is a normal part of digestion. It usually occurs when food isn't completely broken down in the intestine, allowing a build-up of gasses. Much of this gas is absorbed into the blood stream, but some of it becomes flatulence.

While a little flatulence is normal, some dogs are exceedingly gassy. This is usually caused by certain foods, eating too fast, or even a lack of exercise. Whatever the cause, it's usually not that difficult to fight the fumes. To make life more pleasant, here's what experts recommend.

Overhaul her diet. Certain foods—especially those containing soybeans—are notorious gas-producers. When your dog is unusually windy, the easiest solution may be to switch her to a different food, says Stuart Gluckman, D.V.M., a veterinarian in private practice in Mendon, New York. Changing to a food with little or no soy may be all it takes to stop your dog being so gassy.

Every dog reacts to foods differently, Dr. Gluckman adds. You may have to try several foods over a period of months to find one she can tolerate. Just be sure to switch foods gradually, substituting a little bit of the new food for some of the old over a period of days or weeks. Changing diets suddenly can give dogs unpleasant side effects like diarrhea.

Certain foods, including milk, cheese, broccoli, and cauliflower, will cause flatulence in just about any dog. If you've been feeding your pet these foods, you may want to back off for a few days to see if things improve.

Change the protein. Nearly any ingredient in your dog's food can cause flatulence, but it's usually protein that causes the most problems. "Feed her a different type of protein, or a smaller percentage of protein," advises Dr. Gluckman. If her current food gets most of its protein from beef, for example, you may want to switch to a food with a lamb-based protein.

Give more fiber. Adding fiber to your dog's diet will cause food to move more quickly through the intestines, giving gas less time to develop, says Kenneth Harkin, D.V.M., assistant professor in the Department of Clinical Sciences at Kansas State University's College of Veterinary Medicine in Manhattan.

"Try adding Metamucil to your dog's diet," suggests Dr. Harkin. It's very high in fiber and readily available. He recommends mixing Metamucil (or a generic counterpart) in your dog's food with every meal, giving one teaspoon for every 10 to 20 pounds of body weight.

If your dog turns her nose up at the addition of this rather "sawdusty" supplement to her food bowl, more palatable high-fiber foods such as canned pumpkin or green beans may help reduce flatulence, says Dr. Harkin. Just add a little bit, depending on her size, and wait a few days to see if you get results. Be careful not to add too much, or you might unintentionally give your dog diarrhea, since these foods are also used to relieve constipation. Likewise, Dr. Harkin advises to go slowly with any dietary change to prevent intestinal upsets, including more gas.

Bring her insides into balance. The intestines normally contain large amounts of beneficial bacteria, which aid in digestion. But sometimes dogs don't have enough of these bacteria, which can result in flatulence. Giving your dog acidophilus—the same ingredient in live-culture yogurt—will bring the beneficial bacteria back up to healthful levels, says Laurel Kaddatz, D.V.M., a veterinarian in private practice in Fairport, New York. Dogs that don't like liquid acidophilus because of its sour taste will usually enjoy the chewable tablets, he adds. You can give your dog the human dose listed on the label. It usually takes a few days for acidophilus to be effective, says Dr. Kaddatz. Adding plain yogurt (with active acidophilus culture) to your dog's dish might also help—if she'll eat it.

This golden retriever gets a lot of exercise, which stimulates her intestines and helps reduce flatulence.

Slow things down. Dogs that gobble their food swallow a lot of air along with it. And the more air they swallow, the more gas accumulates in their intestines. Vets sometimes recommend placing a large object—one that's too large to swallow—in the middle of your dog's food bowl. She will have to pick around the obstacle in order to get at her food, and this will cause her to eat much more slowly.

Putting a rock in your dog's food bowl will make her eat more slowly and swallow less air, which helps reduce gas.

Another way to encourage your dog to eat at a more sedate pace is to spread her food out thinly on a tray, says Dr. Gluckman. And if there's more than one pet in the family, it's a good idea to feed them separately. Dogs will often eat in a hurry because they're afraid other pets will get to their food before they do.

Head outdoors. Exercise stimulates the intestines and will help remove excess gas from your dog's system. At the same time it stimulates dogs to have a bowel movement, and this will remove even more gas.

FAST FIX To stop gas fast, give your dog a digestive enzyme called CurTail. It goes to work almost immediately. Available from vets, it breaks down sugars in the digestive tract before they lead to gas. Sprinkle a few drops on her food, says Dr. Gluckman. Bean-O, a nearly identical product, is available in pharmacies and grocery stores.

Fleas

They're so small you can hardly see them, but they cause trouble that's way out of proportion to their diminutive size. The American Veterinary Medical Association estimates that fleas and the problems they cause, like itching and hot spots, account for more than half of the skin cases veterinarians treat. When you consider that a single flea can live 6 to 12 months and lay as many as 40 eggs a day, it's no surprise that these little bloodsuckers are the bane of many dogs' existence.

Even if your dog isn't particularly sensitive to fleas, it's worth getting rid of them because they're the leading cause of tapeworms, parasites that take up residence in the small intestine. And for dogs that are sensitive, a single bite can send them into a scratching frenzy.

Don't wait for your dog to start scratching before checking for fleas, says Jody Sandler, D.V.M., a veterinarian in Yorktown Heights, New York. Give him a daily once-over by running your hands or a flea comb through his coat. If you feel something gritty, part the fur and look for particles that resemble coarse pepper—it's the "dirt" fleas leave behind.

Fleas usually set up camp in places that are hard for dogs to reach, like on the base of the tail or behind the ears. Those are the areas to check first when you're on the daily flea patrol.

The tiny common flea is one of the greatest nuisances your dog may have to cope with.

A quick flea check is being incorporated into this beagle's daily playtime. Fleas are hard to see, but you can easily feel and see the reddish-brown dirt they leave behind.

A Combined Approach

In the last few years there's been a breakthrough in flea control. Some new medications can kill and prevent fleas for months at a time. But you still need to fight fleas on all fronts. This means getting rid of fleas your dog already has and making sure they don't return.

Comb them out. Combing your dog once a day with a fine-toothed flea comb will remove adult fleas from his coat, along with the eggs they leave behind, says Laurel Kaddatz, D.V.M., a veterinarian in private practice in Fairport, New York. Get as close to the skin as you can, repeatedly parting the fur with your fingers as you go. To prevent fleas from leaping off the comb onto the carpet—and then back onto your dog—it's a good idea to dip the comb into a bowl of soapy water between each stroke. This will drown any fleas still clinging to the comb.

Fine-toothed flea combs are very effective for removing adult fleas and their eggs.

Wash them away.

Fleas don't hang on very tight, so giving your dog a bath and lathering him well with a pet shampoo will send a lot of them right down the drain. For extra protection, wash him with a flea shampoo, preferably one that contains pyrethrins—a natural insecticide made from chrysanthemums, says Dr. Sandler. Washing your dog in a pyrethrins shampoo will kill fleas on contact, he says. You can also try flea shampoos containing another natural ingredient called d-Limonene. Though they will prove successful in killing some of the fleas, they're usually not quite as effective as the pyrethrins shampoos, says Dr. Sandler.

FAST FIX If you don't have flea shampoo in the house, you can make your own in a few minutes by mixing apple cider vinegar half-and-half with dish detergent. "It's even safe on puppies and kills fleas very effectively," says Stuart Gluckman, D.V.M., a veterinarian in private practice in Mendon, New York.

Bring out the powders and sprays.

Sometimes it takes more than just a good washing to get rid of fleas. Pet supply stores sell a variety of flea powders and sprays. Some contain pyrethrins, which are very safe and effective. You can get a little more oomph with products that contain both an insecticide (to kill adult fleas) and an "insect growth regulator," which destroys the eggs. "It's birth control for fleas," explains Dr. Kaddatz. The insect growth regulators are a common ingredient in flea collars.

When using sprays and powders, be sure to keep them well away from your dog's eyes, ears, nose, and mouth, says Dr. Kaddatz. When treating your dog's face, he recommends spraying the insecticide on a cloth and then rubbing it over your dog's head.

"Because of the 'mess effect,' I prefer sprays to powders," says Dr. Kaddatz. Powders are messy to apply, because they have to be rubbed through the fur down to the skin.

"One handy trick with powders is to enclose your dog up to his head in a bag or pillowcase with the powder inside," says Dr. Kaddatz. "Then fluff up the bag so he is coated with powder. Just brush him to distribute the powder even better and get rid of excess amounts."

Stop the next generation.

The newest products in the flea-control war, such as Program, which is given orally, and Frontline and Advantage, which are applied to your dog's skin, are the most effective ever developed. Program has no effect on adult fleas, but interrupts their life cycle and prevents them from reproducing. Because it doesn't kill adult fleas, Program is often used in combination with other products. Frontline and Advantage kill all fleas outright.

When using Frontline, part your dog's hair and apply it to the back of his neck. It's the one place dogs like this chocolate Border collie can't reach to lick it off.

All these medications are usually used once a month and in some cases can beat the flea problem for good. "These products have changed the way we look at flea control," says Daryl B. Leu, D.V.M., a veterinarian in private practice in Portland, Oregon.

Home Protection

One reason fleas are so hard to stop is that for every one you find on your dog, there may be a hundred more, in one form or another, on the carpet, in the yard, or on his bed. If you don't get rid of all the fleas (and the eggs), they'll jump back on board and start the problem all over again.

The only effective way to stop the cycle is to treat not only your pet, but other pets that come in contact with him. You'll also need to treat your house and yard, says Michael Dryden, D.V.M., Ph.D., associate professor of veterinary parasitology at Kansas State University's College of Veterinary Medicine in Manhattan. "Wash and spray your house from top to bottom," adds Dr. Sandler. "Fleas can infest places in the house where you might not often look, such as under couches or beds."

Suck them up. The most effective way to get rid of fleas and eggs is to vacuum every room in the house, especially in areas where your pet sleeps, says Dr. Dryden. You can remove an enormous number of fleas in just a few minutes. When you're done vacuuming, be sure to throw out the bag even if it's only partly full. Otherwise, all the fleas inside will creep out and you'll have to start again. Vacuum before you treat the house with insecticide. It stimulates the pupae to hatch and then be killed by the spray.

Hit them when they're down. Even if you don't like using chemicals, the only sure way to stop fleas is by using an insecticide or an insect growth regulator—or both—in the house. These products are safe for humans as well as pets. Plus, after the final treatment, they stay active for about 18 months so you don't have to use them very often. They're available at any pet supply house or you can buy them through a pet supply catalog.

You can use either a medicated spray (usually called a premise spray) or a flea "bomb," says Dr. Sandler. Premise sprays are more effective because they can be evenly applied. You'll want to repeat the procedure several weeks later to kill any young fleas that might have hatched since the first round.

Load up the washing machine. Washing your pet's bedding in hot water once a week will kill both fleas and their eggs, says Dr. Sandler. If your dog sleeps on the carpet or on a mattress that's difficult to wash, cover the area with something that's easily washable, such as a sheet or a large towel, he adds. If your dog shares your bed, you may have to wash your bedding, too.

Spread some dust. A great weapon in the fight against fleas is diatomaceous earth, which is also known as chinchilla dust. Available in pet supply stores, chinchilla dust is a microscopic algae that works by attacking and breaking down fleas' waxy coating. This causes the fleas to dry up and die.

Periodically sprinkle the dust on the carpet, furniture and floors. Let it sit for a few days, then vacuum it up. The algae in the dust will stay active for months, says Dr. Gluckman. Just be sure to wear a dust mask and goggles when vacuuming to prevent the tiny particles from getting into your eyes or lungs, he adds.

ESSENTIAL YARD CARE

Fleas are tenacious and very adaptable. They can survive (and thrive) outside just as well as they do in your living room. The only way to keep them off your dog is to get them out of your yard, says Laurel Kaddatz, D.V.M., a veterinarian in private practice in Fairport, New York.

Fleas don't like heat or direct sun, so don't waste time treating sunny spots on the lawn, says Dr. Kaddatz. Concentrate on places where it's cool and dark—under shrubs, for example, or in shady spots under the porch. Treat those areas with an insect growth regulator and an insecticide specifically designed for outdoor use, advises Michael Dryden, D.V.M., Ph.D., associate professor of veterinary parasitology at Kansas State University's College of Veterinary Medicine in Manhattan.

Look for areas with overgrown grass or weeds, or even piles of lumber, which make perfect outdoor homes for fleas. Simply mowing and raking the yard will make it less hospitable, according to Dr. Dryden.

Another way to stop yard infestations is with nematodes—microscopic worms that devour the larvae and eggs of fleas and other insects. You can get nematodes in garden and pet supply stores. Nematodes are both voracious and safe: Once their flea food source runs out, they simply biodegrade.

Heartworm

With their annoying buzz, their insatiable appetite for blood, and the itchy lumps they leave behind, mosquitoes are certainly not a dog's best friend. They're more than just irritating, however. They can also transmit heartworms, dangerous parasites that can literally clog a dog's heart and lungs like strands of spaghetti, making it very difficult for blood to circulate.

It's impossible to protect your dog totally from mosquitoes, but there are ways to keep their numbers under control. In addition, veterinarians recommend taking preventive measures to keep your dog safe. Here's what they advise.

Give early protection. When you live in an area where heartworm exists it's essential to give your dog preventive medicine. That way, even if he gets bitten by an infected mosquito, the medication will kill the heartworms before they mature and cause problems, says Jerry Woodfield, D.V.M., a veterinary cardiologist in private practice in Seattle. "It's a safe, inexpensive investment, and most dogs love the chewable heartworm medication," he says.

It is important to have your dog tested for heartworm before giving him the preventive medication. Your vet will do a simple blood test to determine whether he has heartworm.

"The medications are available from veterinarians, and are usually

CALL FOR HELP

The longer dogs have heartworm, the more difficult it is to treat, so it's essential to catch it early. The warning signs of advanced heartworm infection include coughing, difficulty breathing, and weight loss, says William J. Fortney, D.V.M., a veterinarian in the Department of Clinical Sciences at Kansas State University's College of Veterinary Medicine in Manhattan.

If your dog is already being treated for heartworm, the most important thing you can do is keep him calm and quiet, and not engage in the usual fun and games. This will help prevent heartworms that are killed by the medication from drifting through the blood vessels and forming a clot in the lungs, Dr. Fortney explains.

Heartworm prevention tablets can be fed to your dog like a chewy treat. This boxer has no idea he's taking medicine that will keep him safe from a potentially serious disease.

given monthly," explains Dr. Woodfield. There are additional benefits to giving your dog the medicine. Some heartworm drugs also protect against intestinal parasites. Depending on which heartworm medication you give your dog, it may help to control roundworms, hookworms, and whipworms.

Keep them out. No one wants to keep the windows shut in hot, humid weather, but that's precisely when mosquitoes are thriving. Vets recommend putting up tight-fitting window and door screens to keep the mosquitoes out of the house. And be sure to repair tears in the screens right away. Even the smallest hole makes it easy for mosquitoes to get inside your house.

Treat the yard. It's a good idea to use an outdoor insecticide regularly to keep your dog's yard, kennel, or doghouse mosquito-free.

Keep things dry. Mosquitoes breed in stagnant water—anything from ponds and large puddles to an inch of water in a tin can. It's

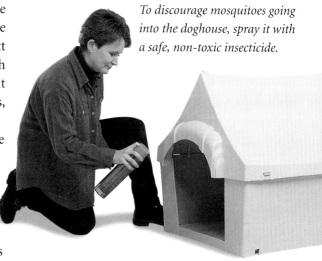

To discourage mosquitoes going into the doghouse, spray it with a safe, non-toxic insecticide.

worth doing everything possible to keep your yard dry—by removing objects that can trap water, for example, or by changing the landscaping to prevent water from collecting. It's also helpful to sweep away small puddles of water before mosquitoes have a chance to move in and start breeding.

Keep him indoors. Mosquitoes are most active in the late afternoons and early evenings when they're looking for food. Try to keep your dog indoors at these times, especially on still evenings, to minimize the risk of bites.

Travel with care. Even if you live where there aren't a lot of mosquitoes and heartworm rates are low, your dog may be at risk when you travel to areas where heartworm is a problem. If he isn't currently taking heartworm medication, talk to your vet before setting out on holiday so you can discuss preventive measures, advises Robert Ridley, D.V.M., Ph.D., professor of pathology at Kansas State University's College of Veterinary Medicine in Manhattan.

FEED THE BIRDS

Purple martins are wonderful garden visitors, not only because they're beautiful to look at, but because they can eat tremendous quantities of mosquitoes, which helps reduce the risk of heartworm infection. Purple martins nest in colonies, so if you want to attract them to your garden, build them a big, condominium-style birdhouse. You can also buy purple martin houses at garden supply stores.

Heat Stroke

Dogs have energy to spare and will happily play as long as you'll let them. But on hot days their exuberance can get them into trouble. Dogs don't have very efficient cooling systems—their only sweat glands are on the pads of their paws. While panting dispels some heat, it isn't enough to keep dogs cool when they really get going. When they push themselves too hard they're at risk of a life-threatening condition known as heat stroke.

All dogs can suffer from heat stroke. Most at risk are elderly dogs, those with a heavy coat, those that are overweight, of large build, heavily muscled, or short-nosed. Dogs with heat stroke pant heavily and feel hot to the touch, says William Fortney, D.V.M., a veterinarian in the Department of Clinical Sciences at Kansas State University's College of Veterinary Medicine in Manhattan. Their lips will stick to their gums and the inner ears will flush. If your dog is unstable on her feet, barely or nonresponsive, or even comatose, you must act at once.

Heat stroke can damage the internal organs and, without fast treatment, can be deadly, says Dr. Fortney. It is always an emergency that must be treated by a vet. It's essential to start lowering your dog's temperature straightaway, even if you can't get to the vet immediately. Then continue the cooling process as you make your way there.

Cool her from the inside out. Dogs with heat stroke are essentially burning up inside. Give them ice cubes to lick to lower their body temperature while also replacing essential fluids. "Even a drop of a few degrees in temperature will increase your dog's chances of recovery," says James Ross, D.V.M., chair of the Department of Clinical Sciences at Tufts University School of Veterinary Medicine in North Grafton, Massachusetts.

Dogs with heat stroke will sometimes lose consciousness very quickly. If she isn't able to lick ice cubes, bathe her paw pads with rubbing alcohol. The rapid evaporation of the alcohol will help dissipate body heat.

Get her good and wet. An efficient way to lower your dog's temperature fast is with cool water. (Don't use cold water, because it could bring on seizures.) You can soak her with the garden hose or pitchers of water. Or, if she's not too heavy, lift her into the bathtub or the kitchen sink and let her soak. Pointing a fan in her direction will speed up the cooling process, says Kathy Gaughan, D.V.M., assistant professor in the Department of Clinical Sciences at Kansas State University in Manhattan.

Keep cooling her. On your way to the veterinarian, keep her cool by placing wet towels on

Cool your dog down with the garden hose. It works quickly, and dogs love the spray.

PREVENTING HEAT STROKE

Heat stroke in dogs can come on quickly, especially in hot weather. And once dogs overheat, cell damage can occur within minutes. So it's essential to always keep them cool. Here's what vets advise.

• Provide lots of water and shade and take it easy. Don't let your dog wear herself out. She may want to run and play on a steamy day, but it's up to you to set limits. During warm months, it's best to exercise and play in the morning and evening, and rest during the mid-day heat.

• Be careful with outdoor restraints. Dogs that are tied outside have a way of getting

tangled. If they get "stuck" in full sun, heat stroke could occur in a hurry.

• When you leave the car to run errands, your dog should leave with you. "Even on an 80°F day, the temperature inside a parked car can reach 130°F in a matter of minutes," says William Fortney, D.V.M., a veterinarian in the Department of Clinical Sciences at Kansas State University's College of Veterinary Medicine in Manhattan. "Leaving a window open a crack won't stop heat build-up, and if you leave it open too far, you risk your dog jumping out while you're gone."

• No matter where you take your dog, be sure to always take water with you. "Stop and offer her a drink every 20 minutes, especially if she's running or working hard," says James Ross, D.V.M., chair of the Department of Clinical Sciences at Tufts University School of Veterinary Medicine in North Grafton, Massachusetts.

• A dog house can turn into an oven in the sun, so make sure it's kept in the shade, along with her drinking water.

her head, neck, chest, and abdomen, says Dr. Gaughan. Use a squirt bottle to keep the towels wet, and continue giving her ice cubes to lick or putting rubbing alcohol on her paw pads. And open the windows or turn the air conditioner on high, which will further help to keep your dog cool and reduce her temperature while you're travelling to your veterinarian.

BREED SPECIFIC

Pekingese, pugs, bulldogs, shih tzus, and other short-nosed dogs run a high risk of overheating. This is because short-nosed dogs pant less efficiently than long-nosed dogs.

Hot Spots

Hen a dog's got an itch, he'll get right to it and give himself a good scratch. While the occasional scratch is harmless, some dogs don't know when to quit. The more they scratch, lick, and bite an itchy spot, the itchier and more irritated it becomes. This can lead to a hot spot, which is always a secondary reaction to another condition.

Hot spots form when bacteria spread rapidly among the hair follicles in the area your dog is scratching, causing bald, circular patches of inflamed skin. "Anything from matted hair and mosquito bites to impacted anal sacs can cause the incessant scratching that leads to hot spots," says William H. Miller, Jr., V.M.D., professor of dermatology at Cornell University's College of Veterinary Medicine in Ithaca, New York.

The amazing thing about hot spots is how quickly they grow, says Jody Sandler, D.V.M., director of veterinary services at Guiding Eyes for the Blind in Yorktown Heights, New York. "A hot spot can grow from the size of a dime to a dinner plate in 12 to 24 hours," he says.

Though hot spots look scary, they only involve the top layer of skin and can heal on their own. In the meantime, you can help them heal more quickly, while also stopping the scratching that caused them to get so bad in the first place.

Clip and Clean

Hot spots go from bad to worse when the hair surrounding the area begins to mat, says Dr. Sandler. The tightly woven fur covers the inflamed area, trapping heat and humidity and creating the perfect setting for bacteria to thrive.

Clipping away hair mats will allow you to clean the area thoroughly. At the same time, it will improve air circulation, which helps hot spots heal more quickly. Hot spots can be very painful, so be prepared to get a reaction from your dog when you go to work, says

A hot spot heals more quickly if it's exposed to the air. Use electric clippers to trim away the hair over and around the hot spot.

Dr. Miller. The gentlest dog may snap when you poke a tender spot, he warns. So give your pet plenty of reassurance, and be prepared to restrain and muzzle him if it's the only way to get the job done.

Clear the area. Use electric clippers to closely crop the hair over and immediately surrounding the hot spot. Don't use scissors because you could easily damage the sensitive skin if your dog moves at the wrong time.

Pick up the hair. To remove hair clippings from the sore, put a water-soluble jelly (such as K-Y jelly) on a gauze pad and press it over the hot spot. When you remove the gauze the hair clippings will come up with it, says Stuart Gluckman, D.V.M., a veterinarian in private practice in Mendon, New York. K-Y jelly washes off easily and completely at bath time.

Wash it well. Dip a soft cloth in warm water and wring it out. Hold it against your dog's skin for 10 minutes to loosen any crusting that has occurred. Then gently wipe the hot spot to finish the cleaning. You can repeat this process two or three times a day.

To kill bacteria, you may want to clean the hot spot with an over-the-counter antiseptic, such as Nolvasan or Betadine. Don't use any product that contains alcohol—the pain will send your poor dog yowling to the moon, says Dr. Sandler.

Air it out. After the hot spot is clean, the best treatment is to leave it alone. Do not put on a bandage as it will only slow the time the hot spot takes to heal, says L.R. Daniel, D.V.M., a veterinarian in private practice in Covington, Louisiana. "You may think you should soothe the area with a moisturizer, but this can make things worse," he says. "Avoid all moisturizers or ointments, even the antibacterial ones. They'll trap the moisture and make things worse. Water-soluble sprays or gels such as aloe vera are fine—they soothe and heal and don't 'cloak' the sore."

One product that can be helpful is Burow's solution. Available from pharmacies, it will help dry the sore. An easy way to apply it is to put the solution in a spray bottle and mist the spot two or three times a day.

CALL FOR HELP

When they're cleaned and well-aired, most hot spots will clear up in a few days without causing serious problems. When they aren't getting better—or are actually getting worse—there's a good chance your dog is developing an infection and you'll need to call your vet.

Even when hot spots don't get infected, the pain is often so severe that dogs will cringe at the slightest touch. If your dog will not let you get near enough to treat the sore, ask your veterinarian to help, says William H. Miller, Jr., V.M.D., professor of dermatology at Cornell University's College of Veterinary Medicine in Ithaca, New York. He will probably numb the hot spot, then give it a thorough cleaning, he explains.

One of the most effective natural remedies for hot spots is the juice of the aloe vera plant. The gel, which is extracted by breaking open a leaf, will soothe and help to heal your dog's hot spot.

Heal it with tea. Tea, which contains tannic acid, will also help the drying and healing process, says Lowell Ackerman, D.V.M., Ph.D., a veterinary dermatologist in private practice in Mesa, Arizona. Make a strong brew of tea and let it stand until it's cool to the touch. Apply a gauze pad soaked in the cool tea directly to your dog's sore spot. Repeat once or twice each day.

Stop the Itching

Since hot spots are almost always caused by scratching, it's worth doing everything you can to find what's causing the itching. If you can figure out what's causing him to itch—and can figure out a way to stop it—you can probably prevent the hot spots from getting started.

Foil the fleas. Dogs that are sensitive to fleas are prime candidates for hot spots, says Dr. Miller. If you suspect your dog has fleas—the telltale sign is tiny, pepperlike specks in the fur or next to the skin—give him a bath right away and shampoo his coat with a pyrethrins-based shampoo. Pyrethrins are natural insecticides that are both safe and effective at stopping fleas. Then talk to your vet about long-term flea-control products, such as Frontline or Advantage. For more on fighting fleas, see page 61.

Ease the aches. Dogs with arthritis or hip dysplasia will often chew or lick at the areas that hurt, which can lead to hot spots. Dogs with joint pain need to be under a veterinarian's care, but you can often ease the pain simply by applying a hot water bottle. Wrap it in a thick towel to prevent burning and apply it to the aching area for a few minutes several times a day. This will ease the discomfort as well as the urge to bite or scratch.

Keep him busy. Dogs are companionable creatures in need of stimulation. "A dog that's bored and lonely will often worry at his skin until it becomes an obsession," says Daryl B. Leu, D.V.M., a veterinarian in private practice in Portland, Oregon. Dogs need regular walks—at least 20 minutes twice a day—as well as lots of play time and regular company. If you keep him busy, says Dr. Leu, he'll have much better things to do than scratch.

Check his coat. Burrs, thorns, grass seeds, and small sticks can work their way into your dog's coat and scratch his skin. It's worth checking his coat carefully when he's been outdoors, parting the fur to see if anything is trapped next to the skin.

Unwrap the mats. Once hair mats have formed, they can be very difficult to remove. But they're easy to prevent by brushing your dog once a day, and taking a few minutes to dry him thoroughly after he bathes or swims.

It's hard to see hot spots on dogs with dense, heavy coats, such as Samoyeds. When they start scratching, take a little time to check the skin. Hot spots are much easier to treat when you catch them early.

BREED SPECIFIC

Any dog can get a hot spot, but long-haired breeds such as golden retrievers, Irish setters, Samoyeds, and bichons frises have the highest risk because their hair is prone to matting.

71

Intestinal Problems

Some dogs are garbage gobblers who can eat almost anything without experiencing anything worse than a loud belch and a little bit of gas. Then there are those delicate souls whose digestive systems revolt at the slightest excuse. In between are the millions of dogs that occasionally get an upset stomach, along with the vomiting or diarrhea that may accompany it, says Caroline Nothwanger, D.V.M., a veterinarian in private practice in Fairfax, Virginia.

Unfortunately, dogs' digestive problems aren't only caused by adventuresome eating. Intestinal parasites are also a common cause of diarrhea. So are food allergies, bacterial and viral infections, and ulcers. Even stress can put your dog's insides in an uproar, says Harriet Lederman, V.M.D., a veterinarian in private practice in Millburn, New Jersey.

Two of the most common causes of dogs' intestinal problems, and the easiest to treat, are giving them rich foods or changing their food too often. Vets recommend giving dogs the same food every day because their intestines can't handle frequent changes. And avoid giving dogs human leftovers because they may be hard for them to digest, says Dr. Lederman.

If your dog keeps getting sick despite your best efforts, here are some additional ways to keep his insides calm.

Raise his culinary standards. Dogs aren't picky about what goes in their mouths, and they'll lap up dirty water as if it were Perrier, and gobble last week's trash as enthusiastically as kibble. "If you have a dog that often has bowel trouble, treat him like you treat yourself," says Terry McCoy, D.V.M., a veterinarian in private practice in Corvallis, Oregon. Give him fresh water every day, and do everything you can to keep him from foraging. The more you control what goes in his stomach, the less you'll have to cope with what comes out, he explains.

Seize the Day

PUPPY DOG TALES

Most dogs will raid the trash when they see the opportunity, but Magic had bigger plans, as her owner, Ginny Debbink of Long Valley, New Jersey, discovered when she came home one day and found the house littered with crumbs, wrappers, and containers.

Magic, a German shepherd who was one year old at the time, had opened every cupboard she could reach, as well as the refrigerator, the bread drawer, the oven, and the dog food container. Missing—and presumably consumed—were five pounds of potatoes, several large onions, two loaves of bread, a bag of potato chips, a large box of saltines, a casserole of lasagna, a pound of butter, a head of lettuce, a bag of carrots, several apples, and about five pounds of kibble.

Not surprisingly, Magic's belly swelled up like a balloon, but she apparently had a cast-iron stomach to match her voracious appetite. The one consequence of her adventure was a bad case of gas, which bothered the people in her family a lot more than it did Magic.

Magic suffered no ill effects from her gluttony, says Debbink, who suspects she'd do it all over if she could.

Give him chicken broth. When your dog is suffering from a bout of intestinal problems, it's important that he continue drinking to prevent dehydration. An easy way to boost his fluid intake is to give him low-fat, low-salt chicken broth, says Karen Mateyak, D.V.M., a veterinarian in private practice in Brooklyn, New York.

Put the cat box in a safe place. Dogs and cats may not always be the best of friends, but dogs often have an unhealthy liking for what kitty leaves behind. "Many dogs raid the cat box regularly with no problem," says Dr. McCoy. But dogs with sensitive stomachs can't handle that kind of snacking. Try putting the cat box on a table or some other place your dog can't reach. Or use a covered box with an opening that is too small to accommodate your dog, suggests Amy D. Shojai, author of *Competability: A Practical Guide to Building a Peaceable Kingdom Between Dogs and Cats.*

Treat him with digestive enzymes. The pancreas produces enzymes needed to digest the nutrients in foods. Some dogs with digestive

CALL FOR HELP

Most intestinal problems clear up fairly quickly, but some never go away. Dogs with a condition called inflammatory bowel disease may be fine for months or even years, and then suddenly have an attack.

Symptoms of inflammatory bowel disease include diarrhea, vomiting, loss of appetite, and a low energy level. If your dog has any of these symptoms for more than a day, call your veterinarian.

problems aren't able to produce enough of these enzymes. Supplementing your dog's diet with digestive enzymes, available in health food stores and from pet supply catalogs, will help him digest his food the way he's supposed to, says Dr. McCoy. Just sprinkle the powder on your dog's food, following the instructions on the package.

Help the medicine go down. Veterinarians often recommend giving aspirin to dogs with arthritis or other joint problems, or for lowering fever. Even though aspirin is quite safe, it can damage the delicate lining of the stomach and lead to ulcers or other kinds of stomach upset. If your dog does need aspirin, be sure to give it to him with meals, which will prevent it from coming into direct contact with the stomach lining. And it's best to use buffered aspirin, which causes much less stomach upset than plain aspirin, says Dr. Mateyak.

BREED SPECIFIC

All dogs have occasional digestive problems, but German shepherds (right), Rottweilers, shar-peis, basenjis, and Lundehunds have a worse problem: They have a high risk of developing inflammatory bowel disease. In addition, German shepherds don't always produce enough digestive enzymes, which can lead to diarrhea.

73

Keep stress levels low. Changes in routine, such as moving to a new house or even getting new furniture, will put many dogs out of sorts, and diarrhea may be the result, says Dr. Lederman. If your dog happens to have a nervous nature, do everything you can to keep his stress levels down, she says. At the very least, try to give him some extra attention when things are more chaotic than usual.

Lock up the garbage. All dogs run the risk of intestinal problems when they scavenge where they shouldn't. Seldom ones for reflection, dogs will often swallow without any regard for the the consequences. Keep all trash cans locked away, including the one in the kitchen, which most dogs are capable of opening.

Teach him to "drop it." Train your dog from an early age to obey your command to "drop it." This will be invaluable if you catch him with a harmful object in his mouth, such as a candy wrapper, a sharp piece of metal, or a stone, which could lead to intestinal problems if he swallows it.

Dogs like this Siberian Husky are sticklers for routine and can become stressed by major changes. To keep their emotions—and their stomachs—calm, a little extra attention can be a big help.

POOCH PUZZLER

Why do dogs eat grass?

No matter how much dogs love their kibble or a scrap or two of meat, they occasionally get a craving for greens, and will contentedly munch on grass or green weeds for as long as you'll let them.

Dogs are omnivorous animals, which means they need plant- as well as meat-based foods, explains Susan Wynn, D.V.M., a veterinarian in private practice in Marietta, Georgia.

More is involved than just nutrition, says Dr. Wynn. Dogs often eat grass when their stomachs are upset, which suggests it plays some sort of medicinal role. "It seems to meet an instinctive need," she says.

In today's world of pesticides and chemical sprays, however, a grass salad isn't always safe for your dog to eat, Dr. Wynn adds. If your dog really seems to crave greens, you should play it safe and give him some clean, fresh vegetables, instead.

FAST FIX One of the best ways to ease diarrhea and other intestinal complaints is to put your dog on a food fast for 24 hours. This will give his system a chance to recover from whatever's making it upset. After the fast, give your dog small amounts of bland food every four hours for a day or two. Good types of bland food you can feed him include equal amounts of boiled, unsalted, unflavored, white rice, and boiled skinless chicken, or boiled hamburger.

Itching

Whether it's the constant jingle of their tags or the thumping of their elbows against the floor, dogs have ways of letting you know they're itchy. It's worth taking note of the ruckus because nonstop scratching can leave skin sore and irritated.

Dogs are naturally itchier than people. They may scratch because of fleas, mites, allergies, dry skin, or simply dirty fur, says Hilary Jackson, B.V.M. & S., assistant professor of dermatology at North Carolina State University College of Veterinary Medicine in Raleigh. The best way to stop the scratching is to find the cause of the itch, and there are ways to give quick relief.

Start with a bath. Without an occasional washing, dirt on your dog's coat will trap oils and other debris next to the skin, making her extremely itchy, says Dr. Jackson. She recommends bathing your dog once a month with a dog shampoo. "Human shampoos can be too harsh and make itching worse," she says.

Soothe it with oatmeal. Oatmeal baths will soothe the skin and help relieve itchiness.

Vets recommend adding colloidal oatmeal (like Aveeno) to the bathwater and letting your dog soak in it for five to 10 minutes.

She may not find bath-time fun, but this cocker spaniel will be glad that the soak eases her itching.

Fight the fleas. Dogs that are allergic to flea saliva can suffer intense itching, says William Fortney, D.V.M., a veterinarian in the Department of Clinical Sciences at Kansas State University's College of Veterinary Medicine in Manhattan. Vets often recommend a medication like Program or Frontline, both of which are very helpful in eradicating fleas. See page 61 for more on flea control programs.

To stop fleas and ease itching right away, give your dog a cool-water bath and wash her coat with a flea shampoo. After the bath, use flea powder or flea spray, which will stop itching while you begin a longer-term program.

Keep the air clean. If your dog has allergies she'll feel itchy when pollen counts are high. Try to keep her indoors during the morning or evening hours, when pollen counts are highest, says Laurel Kaddatz, D.V.M., a veterinarian in private practice in Fairport, New York. For even better allergy protection, he recommends keeping the filters on your furnace and air conditioner clean to reduce the amount of pollen and other allergens coming into the house.

Fix it with fatty acids. Some dogs get relief from allergy-related itching with fatty acid supplements. They are available from health food stores and your vet. They take about six weeks to work. Ask your vet for the right dosage.

Give antihistamines. You can often stop allergy-related itching with an antihistamine like Benadryl, says Dr. Kaddatz. The usual dose is one to three milligrams for every pound of dog. Check the dosage with your vet.

Licking and Chewing Skin

A lick is a pretty effective way for your dog to remove a little dirt from his coat or soothe a scratch. But some dogs don't know when to quit. They'll lick and chew their coats so often and for so long that they'll wear away the fur and damage the skin underneath, sometimes causing sores and infections.

Dogs often lick and chew their skin when they're feeling itchy—because of fleas, for example—or when they're in pain, says Laurel Kaddatz, D.V.M., a veterinarian in private practice in Fairport, New York. They also lick when bored or stressed. If your dog is focusing his energy on one spot, he's probably injured or has a skin infection. More general, all-body licking and chewing may indicate that your dog has an allergy or is anxious.

Whether the irritation is all over your pet's body or all in his head, there are a number of steps you can take to stop the licking and chewing and help his skin to recover.

Begin with a flea patrol. "I don't know how often I've heard an owner say, 'I just know my dog doesn't have fleas,' and sure enough, we usually find one or two," says Jody Sandler, D.V.M., director of veterinary services for Guiding Eyes for the Blind in Yorktown Heights, New York. For dogs that are sensitive to fleas, even one or two bites can send them into a veritable licking and chewing frenzy, he explains.

It's worth taking a few minutes to comb through your dog's coat with a fine-toothed comb called a flea rake, looking for fleas or gritty particles that look like coarse pepper, which are the wastes fleas leave behind, says Dr. Sandler. If you find either, wash your dog well with a flea shampoo, and follow that with some form of ongoing flea control—either a pyrethrins-based powder or spray, or one of the newer products such as Frontline or Advantage. You should also treat your home and yard, preferably with a spray that will kill eggs, larvae, and adult fleas. If the licking and chewing stop, you've probably found the solution. But don't expect this to happen immediately. It may take from five to seven days after treatment for the itching to go away and for your dog to ease off from licking and chewing his skin.

This collie is chewing and licking his paw, which has been cut by a sharp stone.

Divert his attention. When you see your dog chewing or licking himself, distract him by giving him some attention. Then give him something else to chew, such as a rawhide or a chew toy. When dogs are licking themselves because of stress or boredom, this will help lift their spirits and keep their minds off their hides.

When boredom is causing your dog to lick, distract him with a chew treat. A rawhide bone will keep this boxer engrossed for hours.

Check for irritation. Dogs sometimes chew and lick at one particular spot because they're trying to get rid of something stuck in the fur or skin, like a thorn or burr, says Dr. Kaddatz. When you see your dog licking non-stop at one particular area, check to see what's there, he says. If you find a thorn or burr, gently remove it with your fingers or a pair of tweezers. Be careful not to break it off or leave a piece behind in the skin, which will only make the discomfort worse.

Help him heal. Dogs will fuss over any scrape and scratch, and their licking could interfere with the healing process and cause an infection, says Dr. Kaddatz. He recommends washing small scrapes and scratches and then treating them with an over-the-counter aluminum hydroxide preparation, such as those used for diaper rash or poison ivy. (Don't use products that contain zinc, which can be dangerous if your dog licks them off.) Also, apply an antibiotic ointment to prevent infection.

Ease the pain. Dogs with painful conditions like arthritis and hip dysplasia will often lick furiously at the offending spot. When they can't reach the source of the pain, they'll go after the next best thing. For example, a dog might lick at his flank when he can't reach his back, says Daryl B. Leu, D.V.M., a veterinarian in private practice in Portland, Oregon.

Pets with long-term conditions like arthritis always need a veterinarian's care. But you can often relieve the pain—and the chewing—with simple home remedies, such as massaging the sore area for five or 10 minutes at time, or by applying a hot water bottle (wrapped in a towel to distribute the heat and prevent burning) to the areas where he hurts, says Dr. Leu.

Keep allergies at bay. When pollen fills the air and mold spores populate the ground, your dog may go into a frenzy of licking and chewing. The face, feet, and backside are the areas dogs with allergies usually go after, says Dr. Kaddatz. Try keeping your dog indoors as much as possible on days when pollen counts are high, particularly in the morning and evening.

FAST FIX A cool bath gives instant, short-term relief from itching caused by allergies, says Dr. Kaddatz. A spritz of witch hazel spray is another instant soother.

Change his diet. Food allergies can make your dog's skin terribly itchy, causing him to lick and chew incessantly. Dogs with food allergies may also have frequent skin infections. The only way to stop food allergies is to give him a complete change of diet. Find a food that has none of the ingredients that are in his current chow. In particular, look for a different source of protein. This can be a little tricky because most pet foods contain the same kinds of protein, such as poultry, beef, and dairy products, as well as various cereals. Pet supply stores sell hypoallergenic foods that contain "unusual" protein sources, such as fish, venison, or rabbit.

Over a week to 10 days, gradually replace your dog's old food with more and more of the new. (Changing diets too quickly can cause diarrhea.) Once he's switched entirely to the new diet, wait for about 12 weeks. If the chewing and licking disappear, you've probably found the problem, says James Noxon, D.V.M., staff dermatologist at the Veterinary Teaching College of Iowa State University in Ames.

While you're switching to the new diet, be sure to eliminate biscuits and other snacks, which can also contain allergy-causing proteins, Dr. Noxon adds. The same is true of chewable vitamins or heartworm tablets, as well as foods that other pets in your family may be eating. To be safe, you may want to feed your pets separately until you've identified the problem.

Try the buddy system. Loneliness is a common cause of anxiety. "As a pack animal, your dog wants to be with the rest of the pack," explains Dr. Leu. But if the human pack is away much of the day, a dog may direct his anxiety inward, he says. Getting another dog—or at least making regular "play dates" with another dog—is a great way to help prevent licking caused by loneliness. If a canine companion isn't available, the human kind will do. Hire a walker or petsitter to visit your dog while you're away to help reduce his stress and the urge to chew.

Don't fence him in. Dogs can get bored or stressed during long periods of confinement, and they'll sometimes lick and chew as a way of

CALL FOR HELP

Dogs love nothing better than running through gardens and fields, but nature's pastoral places aren't as gentle as they seem. They're often teeming with foxtails, grasslike weeds with sharp little seeds. When the seeds get trapped in your dog's fur, they can burrow into the skin. In rare cases, foxtails travel deep inside the body, tearing tissues as they go, says Laurel Kaddatz, D.V.M., a veterinarian in private practice in Fairport, New York. At the very least foxtails can cause a nasty abscess, he explains.

Foxtails are immensely irritating, and dogs will frantically lick their legs and paws to get them out. It's worth taking a few minutes after walks in the wild to make sure your dog's fur and skin are free of foxtails. If he continues licking and chewing and you're not sure what the problem is, get him to a vet right away, says Dr. Kaddatz. Foxtails can burrow in very quickly, so every minute counts.

coping with their emotions, says William E. Campbell, a dog behavior consultant in Grants Pass, Oregon, and author of *Behavior Problems in Dogs*. Whenever possible, keep your dog active and involved in family activities, he advises. The less time he spends alone, the less likely he is to chew, he adds.

Increase his activity. Dogs have a lot of energy. They prefer to use it to chase balls and trot around the neighborhood with you. Otherwise, they will sometimes direct it inward and start licking and chewing. To stop this happening, try getting your dog out for more walks or games of fetch. When he stays busy, he'll be worn out at the end of the day and will be much less likely to chew, says Dr. Leu.

Protect the skin. Dogs that focus all their licking energy on one spot of skin will sometimes develop serious, raised sores called lick granulomas, which can take a long time to heal. Lick granulomas usually appear on the lower legs between the elbow and the wrist, says Richard J. Rossman, D.V.M., a veterinarian in private practice in Glenview, Illinois. "If you can just keep your dog from chewing at a sore, it will usually heal on its own," he says. You may need to bandage the area or fit your dog with an Elizabethan collar. This will keep him from licking, giving the sore a chance to heal.

MAKING AN ELIZABETHAN COLLAR

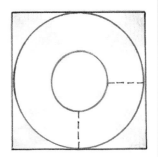

1 In the center of a sheet of stiff plastic or cardboard, mark a circle with a circumference three inches larger than your dog's neck. Outside this circle, mark another with a diameter six inches larger than the first. Cut out the circles and remove a wedge.

2 Cut half-inch slashes around the inside circle and bend back the margin to form a rim. Punch lacing holes on each end of the collar.

3 Insert a lace into the holes and pull together—the circle will become a cone. Put the collar over your dog's head and tie the lace securely.

Lick granulomas can be quite deep and will often get infected, so you'll need to watch the area carefully, says Dr. Rossman. If the sore hasn't healed in two weeks, you'll want to call your veterinarian right away.

Nasal Discharge

You won't see dogs wiping their noses (though they're capable of many things, holding a tissue isn't one of them), but they get drippy just as often as people do, and for some of the same reasons—like allergies, colds, and sinus problems. And because dogs use their noses almost like vacuum cleaners to sniff the exciting things around them, sometimes they suck up things they shouldn't, like grass seeds or even small sticks, which can cause the nose to run.

Most nasal discharges aren't serious, but they can make it hard for dogs to breathe, says Richard J. Rossman, D.V.M., a veterinarian in private practice in Glenview, Illinois. The constant flow of moisture also dries and irritates the nose, and the mucus membranes become very sore. To keep your dog comfortable and turn off the drip, here's what veterinarians advise.

Keep it clean. Dogs with allergies or colds can secrete tremendous amounts of mucus in a day. If you don't remove it right away, it will dry

This collie-German shepherd-mix is having her sore nose soothed with moist baby wipes impregnated with aloe vera.

on the nostrils, making the nose raw and sore. It's worth taking a few seconds periodically to wipe the nose with a warm, damp cloth, says Dr. Rossman. Then dab on a little moisturizer to keep the nose lubricated.

Another way to remove mucus is to use premoistened baby wipes that contain aloe vera, a soothing herbal ingredient that moisturizes the skin and helps it to heal more quickly.

FAST FIX Since dogs with a nasal discharge usually have irritated mucus membranes, you can give them quick relief by taking them into the bathroom with you when you bathe or shower. The steam will instantly soothe the inside of the nose, which will help to reduce the drip later on.

Give an antihistamine. Over-the-counter medications such as Benadryl are very effective for easing allergies that can cause a drippy nose, says Dr. Rossman. Vets usually advise giving dogs one to three milligrams for every pound

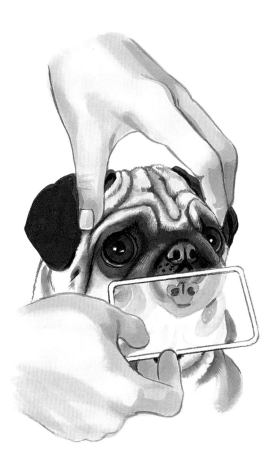

If you suspect there's a foreign body in your dog's nose, hold a small mirror close to the nostrils. If the misting on the mirror is uneven, there is probably something in there and you'll need to take a closer look.

of pet. Individual dogs respond differently to medications, however, so it's a good idea to ask your vet for the precise dose.

Do the mirror test. It's not uncommon for dogs to get small objects stuck in their nostrils, which can cause a copious nasal discharge and a veritable frenzy of head-pawing or nose-rubbing. Take a look to see if something's stuck inside, says Stuart Gluckman, D.V.M., a veterinarian in private practice in Mendon, New York. The easiest way to check for nasal obstructions is to use a small mirror. "When you hold a small mirror under the nose and you don't get equal fogging from both nostrils, you should suspect that there's a foreign body in there," he says.

If you can see the object, you may be able to remove it with your fingers or blunt-nosed tweezers. Most dogs won't hold still for this, however, so ask a friend to hold your dog steady while you reach inside. If your dog keeps squirming or the object is difficult to remove, ask your vet to take a look, says Dr. Gluckman. He should be able to remove the object easily.

CALL FOR HELP

Nasal discharges that are clear and watery are not usually a problem. If the discharge is unusually thick, however, or if it's turning yellow or green, you need to see your veterinarian right away. A thick, discolored discharge is usually a sign that your dog has an infection, and she's going to need antibiotics to clear it up, says Richard J. Rossman, D.V.M., a veterinarian in private practice in Glenview, Illinois.

The smell of the discharge also provides valuable clues, he adds. A dog with an object stuck in her nose will sometimes develop a foul-smelling, pus-like discharge. Your vet will need to clean out the nasal passages and possibly give medications to stop infection, Dr. Rossman says.

Oily Coat

Unless your dog has been rolling in stinky things or having dirt baths, his coat will be shiny and clean. But even the cleanest dogs sometimes get so oily and greasy that they look like they've been working under the car. Dogs naturally secrete a little oil through the skin. Just as naturally, the oil-producing glands are sometimes overactive, causing the skin and fur to resemble an oil slick. And some dogs are simply more oily than others, says Thomas Lewis, D.V.M., a veterinarian in private practice in Mesa, Arizona.

Since an oily coat may signal medical problems—from allergies or parasites to thyroid gland trouble—call your vet if you notice a sudden change in your dog's coat. But in most cases you can easily handle the problem at home. Here's how.

Wash him with a medicated shampoo. Giving your dog regular baths is the best way to keep his coat from getting too oily, says Dr. Lewis. Any pet shampoo will work, but the best products contain selenium or benzoyl peroxide. One popular shampoo, called De-Grease, will quickly remove the oil and also block the growth of yeast, microscopic organisms that thrive on greasy coats.

When bathing your dog, work up a good lather with the shampoo and let it soak into the coat for a few minutes. This gives the active ingredients time to work, says Eileen Gabriel, a dog groomer in Yorktown Heights, New York. Rinse and dry him thoroughly. It's fine to bathe him once a week, she adds.

Try a citrus wash. To remove oil and give your dog a fresh, citrusy smell, wash him with a dog shampoo containing lemon or other citrus oils. "Citrus-based shampoos work well to reduce oils on a dog's coat," Gabriel says.

Soak it up with cornstarch. A quick way to remove oil when you don't have time to give your dog a bath is to brush cornstarch through his fur. Cornstarch is very absorbent and will remove large amounts of oil, Gabriel says. Mix baby powder half-and-half with the cornstarch to give him a pleasant smell. "You can also buy special grooming powders that people who show their dogs use," Gabriel adds. "Most of these are baking soda- or talc-based powders that you work into a dog's coat and then brush out again."

Give him dietary oil. While it may seem contradictory, adding oil to your dog's diet may help to reduce oil on his coat, says Dr. Lewis. He recommends giving oily dogs a little safflower, sunflower, or corn oil with each meal, using anywhere from a teaspoon to a tablespoon, depending on your dog's size. Don't give too much or he may get diarrhea.

BREED SPECIFIC

Dogs that were bred for hunting and retrieving tend to have oilier coats than other breeds. This natural waterproofing helps keep them warm and dry.

Paw and Nail Problems

Your dog's feet are admirably tough. They pad about on gravel, jagged bits of ice, and rough road salt. In summer, there are hot sidewalks, burrs, and thorns to contend with. Most of the time the paws' leathery surface takes whatever nature dishes out. But unlike a pair of sturdy work boots, paw pads can take only so much before they get scraped, raw, or sore.

It's not only pads that are vulnerable. Another potential problem spot is the nails. Your dog's nails grow at a brisk clip, and when they get too long they can crack or tear, says Jody Sandler, D.V.M., director of veterinary services for Guiding Eyes for the Blind in Yorktown Heights, New York. Paw problems can be incredibly painful, Dr. Sandler adds. But they're usually easy to treat at home. In fact, spending just a few minutes a week on basic paw care will keep your dog's feet healthy and strong all year long.

Handling Her Feet

Even dogs that will sit still for brushing and baths often get a little fidgety when it's time to inspect their paw pads or clip their nails. Some dogs, in fact, get a bit frantic, and doing some basic paw care can easily turn into a two-person job, says Daryl B. Leu, D.V.M., a veterinarian in private practice in Portland, Oregon.

Most dogs aren't accustomed to having their feet touched, he explains. The only way to get them used to it is to start slowly. He recommends briefly touching one of your dog's feet, then praising her for letting you do it. If you do

---

P O O C H ❓❓ P U Z Z L E R

Why do dogs hate having their feet touched?

Dogs crave human contact. They'll happily roll over on their backs to get their bellies rubbed or press against your hand for a scratch on the head. But when you reach down to touch their feet, they jerk away as though they'd stepped on hot coals.

This aversion seems to be universal. Even when dogs are playing with other dogs, they usually avoid the feet. Vets aren't sure why so many dogs are foot-shy. Some may be ticklish, especially between the toes. Others may have bad memories of previous—and possibly painful—pedicures, says Eileen Gabriel, a professional dog groomer in Yorktown Heights, New York. Most dogs will put up with a little paw play if you get them used to it when they're young, she adds. Older dogs aren't so flexible, however, so your best bet may be to give attention to other parts of their bodies and leave the feet alone.

---

this several times a day for a few days, she'll get used to the contact and will be less likely to jerk away. Over time, gradually work up to touching two, three, then all four feet. When she's comfortable with that, you can begin touching and manipulating her toes and nails. These are tricky areas, so don't expect instant success, Dr. Leu adds. But if you keep handling her feet, she'll gradually learn there's nothing to fear.

83

Keeping the Pads Healthy

Your dog's paw pads are much tougher than your bare feet, but they aren't immune to painful cuts and sores. The pads' tough, rough surface is only a fraction of an inch thick and is easily cut. And your dog's hairy feet are perfect traps for burrs, irritating moisture, or even jagged spurs of ice. More than any other part of your dog's body, the feet need regular attention—not only to prevent injuries, but to treat them quickly once they occur.

Towel them dry. Unlike human feet, which dry quickly when exposed to air, your dog's furry paws can stay damp for hours at a time. This can damage the skin, says Dr. Sandler, and even attract mosquitoes and fleas. It's worth taking a few seconds to dry the feet thoroughly whenever they get damp. Pay particular attention to the area between the toes, where moisture is most likely to accumulate. A dusting of baby powder will help dry residual moisture.

Apply a little lotion. Dogs that spend a lot of time outside often develop brittle nails and tiny cracks in the pads. In winter, especially, apply a little moisturizer, like Alpha Keri lotion or petroleum jelly, for a few days until the pads are back to normal, says Dr. Leu. Don't do this too often, he adds, because it will make the pads too soft to provide adequate protection.

Soak away the pain. The combination of moisture and everyday wear and tear can make your dog's feet very susceptible to infections, causing the pads to get puffy, red, and sore. A quick way to ease the pain and ward off potential problems is to soak her feet for five to 10

This Staffordshire bull terrier mix isn't crazy about the idea, but getting a foot soak in a water-Betadine solution will reduce the soreness she's experiencing and help prevent infections.

After her foot soak, or anytime she gets her feet wet, dry her feet thoroughly. This will reduce the risk of irritation and infection.

BREED SPECIFIC

Dogs with lots of hair between their toes, such as Samoyeds, Great Pyrenees, and Saint Bernards, run a high risk of foot infections and should have the fur around their feet trimmed regularly. Dogs with relatively hairless feet, like Doberman pinschers and Chihuahuas, don't get a lot of infections. Because they have less protection from the elements, however, they will benefit from wearing booties or having their paw pads treated with a moisturizer.

minutes in a solution of cool water and an antiseptic such as Betadine, says Dr. Sandler. "Ten parts water to one part Betadine is good," he adds. "The solution should look like light tea."

The easiest way to give a foot soak, assuming your dog will stand for it, is to put a few inches of the water and antiseptic solution in a bucket and let her stand with one leg inside. If she won't hold still long enough to soak, wet a washcloth in the solution and clean the pads and between the toes thoroughly. Dry the foot well with a clean towel, Dr. Sandler advises.

Remove the mud. Dogs aren't fussy about where they put their feet, and they'll slog through mud as enthusiastically as they'll run across grass. Wet mud isn't a problem, but when it dries, the rough edges will irritate the paws. Diaper wipes do a good job of removing mud from the paws. And simply washing her feet in warm, soapy water—or, in summer, splashing them with the garden hose—will easily remove the mud before it dries and hardens.

Wash away the salt. Winter is incredibly tough on your dog's paws, not only because the dry air robs them of moisture, but because snow, ice, and road salt abrade and irritate the pads. In addition, salt that dissolves between the toes provides a breeding ground for bacteria. "A dog can get something like jungle rot because of the combination of bacteria, salt, and moisture," says Dr. Sandler.

It's inconvenient to wash your dog's feet after every walk, but it's the only way to protect them. One way to make it a little easier is to keep a bowl or bucket of water near the front door. This way you can give her feet a quick dip whenever she comes inside.

Trim the fur. Even though your dog's coat provides protection from the elements, hair on the feet traps moisture and prevents air from circulating. Trimming the hair between the toes

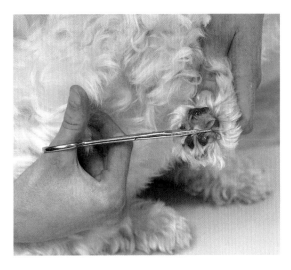

Wet feet cause problems for long-haired breeds, like this Maltese. To trim the hair, spread the toes and cut the fur between them, following the line of the toe.

85

keeps the feet drier and healthier, especially in long-haired breeds like golden retrievers, Maltese, or many of the spaniels, says Dr. Sandler.

Lift one foot at a time and spread the toes with your fingers. "Using blunt-nosed scissors, follow the line of the toe, cutting straight down rather than across," says Eileen Gabriel, a professional dog groomer in Yorktown Heights, New York.

Trim the skin. Tough as they are, paw pads sometimes lose a little skin when dogs run on hard surfaces. "They can actually shave off the surface of the pad," says Dr. Sandler. If you notice a bit of skin hanging loose, you'll need to trim it off. "This makes people a little squeamish, but the very top layer of pad has no nerve tissue in it," he says. "It's better to remove it than to have it flapping and tugging."

Once you've removed the loose skin, clean the pad well. It will usually heal within two to four weeks, says Dr. Sandler. In the meantime, keep your dog on soft surfaces until the skin has a chance to grow back.

Invest in some footwear. Dogs that spend a lot of time outside in harsh weather often need extra protection. Pet supply stores sell a variety of booties that can help protect your dog's feet both in winter and summer, says Laurel Kaddatz, D.V.M., a veterinarian in private practice in Fairport, New York. Most dogs are reluctant to wear them, at least at first, he adds. You can get them used to the idea by putting the foot-

Hold your dog's paw firmly when you are trimming her nails. Using sharp trimmers will prevent the nail from splitting and cracking and make the whole process go a little easier.

wear on their feet for just a minute or two, once or twice a day. If you do this every day for a few weeks, leaving the booties on for longer and longer periods of time, they'll soon get used to them, just as they got used to wearing a collar.

Do a daily foot check. Because your dog's feet are in contact with the ground more than any other part of her body, it's important to check them frequently, says Dr. Kaddatz. "Dogs step on nails, and they pick up thistles and thorns in their wanderings," he says. "You'll want to remove these before they cause further injury or an infection."

When you do have to remove an object from the paw, be sure to clean the area thoroughly and dab on a little antibiotic ointment when you're done, Dr. Kaddatz adds.

Basic Nail Care

Humans have it easy. Even though we tear a fingernail now and then, at least we're not running around on our hands. For dogs, however,

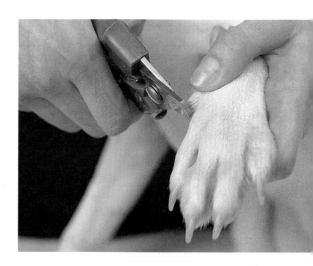

the nails are always banging on the ground or, worse, snagging on carpets. Nails that pull loose from the skin can be excruciatingly painful. Even the minor pressure caused by nails clicking on concrete can make a dog's feet sore.

Dogs that walk on pavement or other rough surfaces automatically get a nail trim with every step, and regular clipping may be less of an issue. Some dogs have slow-growing nails that never cause any problems. But for other dogs, you have to keep their nails trimmed. Here's how to do it.

Do a clip and file. Pet supply stores sell a variety of nail trimmers. It's important to get the right size and style for your dog because using the wrong ones can cause the nails to split, says Gabriel. Even if you already have nail trimmers at home, you may want to consider getting new ones. To work efficiently, trimmers must be very sharp. When they're dull, you'll have to put more pressure on the nail, which can be painful for your pet, she says.

Start by trimming the nail halfway between the tip and the "quick," the place where the vein begins, says Gabriel. In dogs with dark nails, it's not always easy to tell where the quick begins. If you're not sure, it's better to trim off just a little bit at a time. Cutting the nail too close to the paw will damage nerve endings, and your dog will let you know this isn't how it's supposed to be. Cutting the quick can also cause a lot of bleeding, Gabriel warns.

If you do cut too close and the nail starts to bleed, you can stop it fast with a little styptic powder. Or press the nail into a piece of very soft soap, Gabriel says. There's no need to rinse the soap off—it will wear off by itself. Finally, file down any rough edges with an emery board.

Mend the damage. It's not uncommon for dogs to damage their nails—either by pulling them loose on something or just by hammering them on hard surfaces. Split nails usually aren't a problem, says Dr. Sandler. All you need to do is trim the nail as far as you can without cutting into the quick. Your dog's nail will soon regrow as one piece, he says.

Nails that have torn loose are much more serious. They're not only painful, but have a high risk of getting infected. You'll need to take her to your vet, who will probably remove the rest of the nail, using an anesthetic to ease the pain, says Dr. Sandler. "Keep the area bandaged to protect it from dirt and moisture until the new claw grows in," he says. "Her foot will be a little tender for a while, so hold off on Frisbee games and long runs until she's obviously comfortable with putting pressure on it again."

Poisoning

Dogs have wide-ranging appetites, and garden plants, yard chemicals, and even bottles of cough syrup can be as appetizing to them as a bowlful of kibble. Unfortunately, their common sense isn't as well developed as their tastebuds, which is why many dogs in the United States are treated for poisoning every year. The most common causes of poisoning are pesticides and human medications.

Pesticides, which include insecticides, rodenticides, and herbicides, are often carelessly stored. "People leave bags or boxes of lawn care products in the garage, and dogs can easily rip into them," says Steve Hansen, D.V.M., a veterinary toxicologist and director of the ASPCA National Animal Poison Control Center in Urbana, Illinois. Human medications are the second most common cause of poisoning because they, too, are often left within easy reach. "A child-proof cap is no obstacle at all to a nosy one-year-old Labrador," says Dr. Hansen.

Many dogs are attracted to the widely-used plastic roach and ant traps, but these don't pose a serious hazard because they contain only very small amounts of poison, says Dr. Hansen. Though it is best to keep them out of your dog's way, a short bout of vomiting and diarrhea is all they'll cause.

Serious poisoning is scary. It happens quickly and the symptoms can be wide-ranging, depending on the poison. Truth is, by the time symptoms appear you may have only a few minutes to save your dog's life, says Kenneth Harkin, D.V.M., assistant professor in the

Dogs are naturally inquisitive, like this German shepherd-cross. They also tend to sample anything they find, so keep all household cleaners locked away.

Department of Clinical Sciences at Kansas State University's College of Veterinary Medicine in Manhattan.

Poisoning is always an emergency that needs fast attention. Try to speak with your vet quickly before you drive to the clinic to find out if you should do anything at home, advises Stuart Gluckman, D.V.M., a veterinarian in private practice in Mendon, New York. "Minutes can make a big difference," he says.

Sometimes what you do before you go to the vet can be just as important as what happens once you're there, says Dr. Harkin. Here's what veterinarians advise.

Identify the poison. The more information you can give your veterinarian, the more quickly he'll be able to start giving your dog the appropriate treatment. So it's worth trying to figure out what your dog has gotten into.

• **Smell his breath**. Petroleum products like gasoline and kerosene have a very strong and distinctive odor that you'll be able to smell on your dog's breath.

• **Check for bleeding**. Dogs that are bleeding from the mouth, nose, or anus may have swallowed rat or mouse poison. This is because these products contain warfarin, a chemical that causes bleeding.

• **Look in his mouth**. If the gums and lips are bright red, he may have been exposed to carbon monoxide.

• **Search for the source**. Quickly check the house and yard for the shredded remains of packages that may have held something poisonous. Check the bathroom and also your purse to see if any medications are missing.

• **Check the ground for chemical spills**. Dogs will often lap up extremely hazardous substance from puddles on the ground, like antifreeze, for example.

• **Check the pantry**. Some human foods—especially chocolate—are poisonous for dogs. Baking chocolate contains very high levels of a toxic (for dogs) compound called theobromine. As little as four ounces of baking chocolate can poison a 30-pound dog.

Bring along the evidence. When you're pretty sure what your dog swallowed, pack up the remaining substance—or the package it came in—and take it with you to the vet. Product labels include vital information about ingredients and, in some cases, first-aid treatment. At the very least, giving your vet this information ahead of time will allow him to get ready before you arrive.

Poisoning doesn't always cause vomiting, but when it does, be sure to scoop up a sample and put it in a plastic bag. Your veterinarian may need to analyze it to figure out what, exactly, your dog consumed.

Phone the poison experts. Dr. Gluckman suggests dog owners get the number of a 24-hour national animal poison control center from their veterinarian and keep it in a readily accessible place.

Vital assistance can be given over the phone if your dog starts showing signs of poisoning in the middle of the night. The nearest emergency veterinary clinic may not be that close and you don't want to waste time. If you don't know what's caused the problem, an adviser at the center will be able to talk you through the possible options that correspond to the symptoms your dog is displaying. And they will tell you if you should induce vomiting or try to neutralize the poison.

Purge the poison. The best first-aid for many types of poisoning is to help your dog vomit, says Dr. Gluckman, but only if:

1. You're sure the poison was swallowed within the hour.

2. You're certain the poison was not a strong alkali, acid, or petroleum product.

3. Your dog is conscious and alert.

The easiest way to induce vomiting is to give your dog hydrogen peroxide (a three-percent solution), using about one tablespoon per 15 to 20 pounds of your dog's body weight. For a

PRETTY BUT POISONOUS

Some dogs can't resist licking the leaves of household or garden plants, or munching on the occasional flower. Rarely, though, do they eat enough to cause anything more troublesome than a mild attack of vomiting and diarrhea—nature's way of flushing out toxins. Mistletoe and poinsettia are sometimes the culprits in these cases.

The truly hazardous plants are dumbcane, oleander, and sago palm. Dumbcane causes swelling of the throat and possibly suffocation. Oleander contains a chemical similar to digitalis. It can damage the heart and even small amounts can be deadly. Sago palm can be harmful because its nuts can cause liver damage.

Lethargy and vomiting are the first symptoms, and your dog needs to be treated by a veterinarian right away to prevent further damage.

Poinsettia

Dumbcane

50-pound dog, this would be about 2½ tablespoons, says Dr. Gluckman.

Draw the liquid into a needleless syringe or turkey baster and insert the tip into the side of your dog's mouth behind the canine tooth. Release the liquid slowly—if your dog gags, you're going too fast, says Dr. Harkin. Most dogs will vomit within five minutes. If it doesn't work the first time, try it again. If your dog still hasn't vomited, don't do anything else until you get to your veterinarian.

Cool the burn. Even though many types of poisoning are best treated by helping your dog vomit, in some cases it makes things worse. For example, you don't want induce vomiting if your dog has swallowed drain cleaner, kerosene, or other harsh substances because this will cause a "double burn"—once when the poison went down and again when it comes back up, says Dr. Gluckman. A better strategy is to neutralize the chemicals in the stomach, and also soothe the painful burning in the throat and stomach.

"Try to give your dog milk or raw eggs when inducing vomiting is not an option," advises Dr. Gluckman. Or you can give Milk of Magnesia, using one teaspoon for every five pounds of your dog's weight.

No dog will readily lap up any of these substances, particularly when they're sick, so you'll need to use a turkey baster or needleless syringe. The amount you give isn't important—even a small amount will help soothe the burn.

Prostate Problems

For male dogs, the prostate gland is both a blessing and a curse. Located at the base of the bladder, it adds fluid to the sperm, which is essential for reproduction. As dogs age, however, the prostate gland often gets larger and begins pressing on the urethra or the large intestine. It's also prone to infection, which can make urinating painful.

Dogs with prostate problems often need to urinate frequently, and they may cry until they're done. They may also walk a little stiffly to reduce the painful pressure caused by the swollen prostate gland.

The best way to prevent and treat prostate problems is to have your dog neutered. But there are also things you can do at home to keep him a little more comfortable.

Give him time. When the prostate gland is swollen or infected, it often presses on the urethra, the tube through which urine flows. This means that dogs need a lot more time to urinate. They'll also need more opportunities to urinate, since it's difficult for them to finish all at once. So plan on taking your pet outside much more often, and be prepared to wait a bit while he finishes his business.

Soften the stools. Dogs with prostate problems may have trouble having a bowel movement when the gland presses against the large intestine. Give your dog a little oat bran or canned pumpkin, both of which are high in fiber, to soften his stools and make them easier to pass, says Rance Sellon, D.V.M., assistant professor in the Department of Veterinary Clinical Sciences at Washington State University in Pullman. Or you can add a little Metamucil to his food, he adds. If he's still constipated, your vet may recommend using a prescription stool softener to get him regular again.

Get him drinking. Dogs with prostate problems sometimes get urinary tract infections because the trapped urine in the bladder provides a breeding ground for bacteria. Encourage your dog to drink more so that the urine will be

Offer your dog some water during his walk, when he has unlimited opportunities to urinate. This will help to flush stale urine out of his bladder.

less concentrated and infections less likely to take hold, says Shelly Vaden, D.V.M., associate professor of internal medicine at North Carolina State University's College of Veterinary Medicine in Raleigh. Drinking more water will also cause him to urinate more, which will help to flush away bacteria before they cause problems.

Dogs with prostate problems may be reluctant to get up to go for a drink, so put the bowl where it's easy for your dog to reach. It's also

Because this boxer is in pain and reluctant to get up, his owner brings the drink to him.

helpful to encourage him to drink before you go for a walk and again when you come back in. Dogs don't need gallons of water, but sometimes just a gentle reminder that it's there will entice him to lap up a little more.

Take it easy. Prostate problems can be painful and most dogs won't want to run around too much. While some exercise is good and can help ease constipation, for example, too much may be uncomfortable. So keep the walks gentle and slow until he's feeling better.

Relieve the pain. Veterinarians often recommend buffered aspirin for easing prostate pain. Give 10 milligrams of buffered aspirin for every pound of dog, up to three times a day, says Stuart Gluckman, D.V.M., a veterinarian in private practice in Mendon, New York. "It is better to give it with a little food, which will help to prevent stomach upsets," he adds.

In some cases your vet may recommend a prescription pain reliever called Rimadyl. "It has fewer side effects than aspirin, and causes fewer cases of tummy trouble," says Dr. Sellon.

CALL FOR HELP

The prostate gland typically enlarges very slowly, so most dogs won't have problems until middle age or beyond. On the other hand, prostate infections can come on very suddenly. And once prostate infections get started, they can quickly cause whole-body problems, so it's important to call your vet at the first sign of a problem.

Dogs with a prostate infection, prostatitis, will urinate more frequently, although relatively little urine will come out. There may be blood in the urine as well, says Rance Sellon, D.V.M., assistant professor in the Department of Veterinary Clinical Sciences at Washington State University in Pullman.

Most prostate problems occur in intact dogs, Dr. Sellon adds. "So it makes sense to neuter your dog if you don't have plans to show him or breed him."

Shedding

If you've ever spent hours sweeping the floor and vacuuming dog hair from upholstery and carpets, you know that shedding is a normal, if annoying, part of owning a dog. The housework never goes away entirely because shedding is nature's way of making room for new hair. And it doesn't matter what kind of dog you own. Except for the hairless breeds, all dogs shed, whatever their coat type.

Most dogs do their shedding in the spring and fall in response to changing amounts of light, says Lowell Ackerman, D.V.M., Ph.D., a veterinary dermatologist in private practice in Mesa, Arizona, and author of *Skin and Haircoat Problems in Dogs*. Dogs that spend most of their time indoors, on the other hand, may shed all year round because the lighting in your house, unlike light from the sun, doesn't change from season to season.

Even though you can't stop your dog shedding, there are a number of ways to keep your dog's coat—and the house—a little neater. Here's what experts advise.

Brush it out. The best way to control shedding is to brush or comb your dog every day, which will remove surplus hair before it hits the carpet. "Try to get him used to being brushed at a young age so that it becomes a pleasant experience," says Jody Sandler, D.V.M., director of veterinary services at Guiding Eyes for the Blind in Yorktown Heights, New York. Different breeds have different coat types, so it's important to choose the right brushes and combs. A combined approach—brushing your dog followed by a thorough combing—will remove tremendous amounts of hair, he explains.

Slicker brushes and metal combs are very useful on most dogs' coat types, says Cari

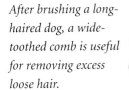

After brushing a long-haired dog, a wide-toothed comb is useful for removing excess loose hair.

Use the pin cushion side of this soft bristle with pin cushion brush on short- or wire-haired dogs.

A slicker brush is useful for most coat types. It will capture plenty of loose hair with each stroke.

A shedding glove is good for removing loose hair after brushing most coat types.

Mayer, a dog groomer in Greenwich, Connecticut. "Shedding rakes are good for removing the loose undercoat of long-haired breeds." But don't begin a grooming session with a rake if your dog hasn't been groomed in a while, she cautions. Pulling out tangled, matted hair with a rake can really hurt your dog. "Shedding gloves, or even just regular rubber gloves, are very good for removing loose hair on short-haired breeds like labs or pugs," Mayer says.

CALL FOR HELP

Most dogs occasionally shed more than usual. During pregnancy, for example, hormonal changes can cause dogs to lose tremendous amounts of hair. And some dogs may shed a lot one week and almost nothing the next. "It's just a variation of what's normal for them," says Lowell Ackerman, D.V.M., Ph.D., a veterinary dermatologist in private practice in Mesa, Arizona.

But there's a big difference between the occasional heavy shedding and shedding that's so severe that your dog develops bare patches in his coat. "Patchy hair loss that doesn't grow back could be a sign of mange," says Hilary Jackson, B.V.M.&S., assistant professor of dermatology at North Carolina State University College of Veterinary Medicine in Raleigh. Dogs with hormone imbalances can also experience heavy hair loss. Don't wait for it to get better. Call your veterinarian right away.

Use short strokes. Your dog's coat is much thicker than human hair, and the long brushing strokes people use for brushing their hair won't work for controlling shedding on dogs. Instead, use firm, deep, short strokes, which will penetrate all the way through the coat. Brush in the direction that your dog's hair grows, working from the head backward to the tail. When you're finished, give your dog another brushing by going against the grain. This will remove any hair that was left behind the first time around.

Schedule regular bath times. Getting your dog good and wet before using a grooming rake or comb makes it possible to remove clumps of loose hair that are easy to collect and throw away later. Be sure to brush out any mats in his coat before wetting your dog. Otherwise the mats will pull together, making them harder to remove later on.

Head for the Hoover. Some dogs won't sit still for it, but vacuuming is a very good way to remove loose hair, says Dr. Ackerman. "Try the fairly quiet, low-powered types of vacuum cleaners." Pet-grooming attachments for vacuum cleaners are available from pet supply stores and through mail-order catalogs.

This Old English sheepdog-Border collie-cross doesn't object to being vacuumed with a small hand-held unit that operates quietly on batteries.

Skin Infections

I t does a great job protecting him and keeping his body temperature constant, but your dog's skin isn't armor-plated. Considering what it has to put up with, that's a pity. Always exposed to the elements, the skin is vulnerable to all sorts of infections from bacteria, viruses, and fungi.

Skin infections are among the most common conditions vets treat. They're a problem for owners, too, and not only because they're concerned about their dogs' health. A number of skin conditions that affect dogs, like ringworm and scabies, are also contagious to the human members of the household. That's why identifying problems—and dealing with them fast—is so important.

Skin infections are usually easy to spot because the skin will look sore and red. Or your dog may be itchy, losing patches of fur, and there may be a bad smell, as well. But even when you know your dog has an infection, it isn't always easy to tell what kind it is. You'll need to see your veterinarian to find out for sure what's going on. Once you know what's causing the problem, however, there are things you can do to help the healing.

This cocker spaniel may have had fun in the mud, but the dirt on his coat is a breeding ground for bacteria.

itching and sometimes sores, says Daryl B. Leu, D.V.M., a veterinarian in private practice in Portland, Oregon. Bacteria also thrive when there's a lot of dirt or oil next to the skin, or when friction—usually in areas of loose skin—provides an opportunity for bacteria to colonize. There are many kinds of bacterial infection, but there is one you may have to deal with—skin-fold infection—that is among the easiest to treat.

Bacterial Infections

Most skin infections are caused by a bacterium known as staphylococci. Staph normally live on the skin and don't cause any trouble at all. When the immune system is weaker than usual, however, staph can suddenly thrive, causing

Skin-Fold Infections

Dogs such as Chinese shar-peis are bred to have enormous folds of loose, floppy skin all over their bodies. Others, such as pugs and bulldogs, have frowny, jowly faces. Unfortunately, this crinkly appearance attracts more than smiles and compliments. These dogs are prone to skin infections because bacteria thrive in the warm, moist areas inside the folds. "Skin isn't really intended to cope with folds like that," says Dr. Leu. "Since bacteria thrive on heat and moisture, you need to cool and dry the skin," he says.

Dry inside the folds. Air has a hard time circulating inside skin folds, which means any moisture that gets inside tends to stay there, attracting bacteria and also irritating the skin. Any time your dog gets wet, use a cloth to dry inside all the "trapped" areas, he advises.

Add some powder. It's not only moisture that's a problem in skin folds, but the friction of skin against skin. Dr. Leu recommends rubbing a little cornstarch in the folds to minimize the chafing. Or you can use a medicated powder like Gold Bond or Desinex. Don't use scented talc powder because the chemicals may irritate your dog's skin.

FAST FIX A quick way to remove moisture from inside skin folds is to apply a little rubbing alcohol. Hold the area so it stays open to the air for a minute, then let it fold naturally again. Don't use it near the eyes or if the skin is inflamed because it will sting.

BREED SPECIFIC

Chinese shar-peis (left), bulldogs, pugs, and Pekingese are prone to skin-fold infections, as are screw-tailed breeds, such as Boston terriers.

Ringworm

Dogs are prone to a number of fungal infections, but the one they get most often is ringworm, which can be transmitted by cats, rodents, or even moist soil. It's called ringworm because the infection causes ring-shaped patches on human skin.

A number of skin problems resemble ringworm, so the only way to be sure that's what your dog has is to take him to the vet. Once you know what you're up against, ringworm takes at least six to eight weeks to treat.

Trim the fur. Cutting the hair surrounding a patch of ringworm makes it harder for the fungus to spread, since the fungus thrives on the hair itself. It also makes it easier to treat with medications, says William Fortney, D.V.M., a veterinarian in the Department of Clinical Sciences at the Kansas State University's College of Veterinary Medicine in Manhattan.

Fight the fungus. There are a number of antifungal creams, liquids, and ointments available over the counter and from your vet. Whichever treatment you use, you'll need to rub the medication on the infected skin once a day for six to eight weeks. For more serious cases of ringworm your vet may recommend a medicated dip or powerful antifungal drugs that are taken orally. Usually you will bathe and dip your dog at the beginning of the treatment and at the end, six to eight weeks later. While you can purchase antifungal dips from a pet supply store, check first with your vet to make sure the one you get will be effective for your dog. You'll need to keep treating him even after the sores have healed because he could still be contagious.

Do a thorough housecleaning. The fungus that causes ringworm is extremely hardy and can survive for up to a year on strands of hair in the carpet, on furniture, or under baseboards, says Dr. Fortney. The only way to prevent your dog from getting reinfected is to be extremely scrupulous about keeping the house clean, and disposing carefully of any hair you have trimmed from your dog. Vets advise sweeping or vacuuming the house at least twice a week while your dog is being treated. It's also helpful to mist the air with an antifungal chemical called chlorhexidine, diluting one ounce in a gallon of water. You can also use the mixture to wash vinyl or hardwood floors.

Steam-clean the furniture. If your dog's favorite spot is a chair with a fitted, unremovable cover, you'll need to have it professionally steam-cleaned. "You may not get the water hot enough if you use a do-it-yourself cleaner you rent at the grocery store," says Dr. Fortney. "The temperature has to be 140°F to kill the fungus."

FAST FIX An easy way to kill the ringworm fungus is to wash your dog's bedding, rugs, and anything else he comes into contact with in very hot water and detergent, along with a mild bleach solution. Plan on doing the wash once a week until several weeks after he's better.

Don't forget the cats. One form of ringworm is commonly transmitted from cats to dogs. Even if your cats don't have any sign of it, they could still carry and spread it. Treat your cats at the same time as you're treating your dog. Be sure to check with your vet before using ring-

Dogs that have been cured of ringworm can get reinfected by contaminated bedding, so it's important to wash sheets, towels, and other bedding supplies in hot water once a week.

worm medications on cats, however. Products that are safe for dogs may be dangerous for cats.

Parasites

Skin infections caused by parasites such as fleas and skin mites are very common, says Dr. Fortney. Many dogs get skin mites at some time in their lives, a type of infection known as mange. There are three types of mange: Demodectic, scabies, and walking dandruff. Each can make life pretty miserable for your dog. And scabies can be passed to humans as well. Most mites cause similar symptoms, but they aren't quite identical.

• **Demodectic mange.** Usually picked up by puppies when they're nursing, this type of mite lives in the hair follicles and doesn't greatly disturb dogs. In warm, moist weather, however, the mites can suddenly multiply and cause red, inflamed skin and some hair loss from the face or front legs. When an older dog gets this type of mange, it often means his immune system is a little weak and that's why the mites have proliferated, says Dr. Fortney. The only practical way to treat the mite infection is long-term drug therapy from your veterinarian.

In healthy pups, demodectic mange will often go away on its own. If the hair loss and inflammation seem minor and don't bother him, give it a month to heal. If it doesn't get better or it gets worse, take him to your vet.

- **Scabies.** This type of mange often appears on a dog's elbows and ears. It's been called "mad itch" because of its intensity. "A dog will simply not stop scratching," says Dr. Leu. "Sometimes he won't even be able to sleep, it gets so bad." Scabies is contagious to humans, so wash your hands after handling your dog.

Start by giving your dog a dip. You will need a fairly potent insecticide from your vet to get rid of the mites," says Dr. Fortney. Ask your vet if the lime-sulfur dip called LymDyp will be effective for your dog. Scabies is highly contagious so it's not enough to dip only the dog who's infected. Treat all the pets in your family. Make sure that the dip you use is safe for other pets.

- **Walking dandruff.** This type of mite multiplies to such large numbers that it can make skin flakes in your dog's coat appear to move— hence its name. Vets don't worry much about walking dandruff because it's only mildly itchy and is easily treated with common flea medications. To make sure what you're dealing with is

A T-shirt prevents this miniature fox terrier from worrying at his itchy skin.

indeed *Cheyletiella*—walking dandruff— and not a seborrheic condition, look directly at your dog's skin with a magnifying glass, says Dr. Leu. "If the skin is moving, it's walking dandruff."

"Regular flea shampoos will knock walking dandruff mites out," says Dr. Leu. Bathe your dog once a week for about three to six weeks to make sure the mites are gone.

Except for demodectic mange in adult dogs, which is always treated by a vet, mange will often go away within a few weeks or months with the right treatments. To help your dog cope with the discomfort in the meantime, there are a few things you can do.

Soothe the itch. Giving your dog weekly baths in cool water and washing him with an oatmeal shampoo will help ease the discomfort caused by mites, says Dr. Leu. It's a good idea to continue the baths for four to six weeks.

Cover them up. Dogs with mange, especially scabies, will often scratch like crazy, breaking the skin and possibly causing another infection. To stop the damage, put a stretch baby suit on your dog, says Dr. Leu. He'll still scratch, but the material will protect his skin from his claws. For big dogs, a T-shirt is a good choice, he adds.

Clean the house. Even though the scabies mite doesn't live long when it's off its host— only about one to two weeks—Dr. Fortney still favors a thorough house-cleaning. Regular vacuuming and sweeping will remove any mites waiting for a ride on a human or animal host.

Skunk Spray

Skunks are masters of self-defense. Their very effective weapon is an oily, highly odoriferous sulfur-alcohol fluid that is secreted from two glands near the anus. Skunks' ability to hit their target is of Olympic status: Gold-medal pinpoint accuracy up to nine feet; bronze-medal occasional accuracy up to 16 feet. The stink can go the distance, too: It can be detected up to half a mile away.

If not treated immediately, a skunked dog will smell for weeks until the oils wear off naturally. Some long-haired dogs can retain the odor for years, smelling every time they get wet. "Whatever you do, get to the spray before it dries on your dog's coat," says Eileen Gabriel, a dog groomer in Yorktown Heights, New York. "Once it dries, you're in for a long, hard task."

Here's what experts recommend to help keep your dog's hair on, quell the smell, and get him back on society's A list as soon as possible.

Wash his eyes. Dogs invariably approach skunks face first, which means they usually take a direct hit in the eyes. The spray isn't toxic, but it can be extremely irritating, says Laurel Kaddatz, D.V.M., a veterinarian in private practice in Fairport, New York. It's important to flush his eyes with an over-the-counter eye wash or saline solution like that used by contact lens wearers. Tap water will do, but saline solution has better soothing properties, says Dr. Kaddatz. Even if no one in your family wears contact lenses, it's worth keeping a large bottle of saline handy.

If your dog keeps scratching at his eyes or continues to squint an hour after the rinsing,

you should call your veterinarian, advises Dr. Kaddatz. Dogs can give themselves corneal ulcers by repeatedly trying to wipe out the skunk spray from their eyes.

Neutralize the spray. One of the best ways to get rid of the stink is to neutralize it with a solution made by mixing two pints hydrogen peroxide, a quarter-cup baking soda, and two or more teaspoons of dishwashing liquid. Hydrogen peroxide is one of the ingredients chemists use to neutralize knock-down smells, explains Stuart Gluckman, D.V.M., a veterinarian in private practice in Mendon, New York.

Start by washing your dog with his regular shampoo, says Dr. Gluckman. (It's a good idea to wear latex or rubber gloves to keep the oily spray off your hands.) After rinsing him well, lather him up again, this time with the homemade shampoo. Work the solution into his coat

hydrogen peroxide

tomato juice

dishwashing liquid

baking soda

vanilla extract

latex gloves

CALL FOR HELP

Even though skunks are best known for the strength of their spray, public health officials have another concern: In some parts of the country skunks are the main carrier of rabies.

Skunks are shy animals that prefer to be left alone. A skunk with rabies, however, can be unusually aggressive and will attack other animals, including dogs, that get in their way. Be especially wary if you see a skunk wandering about during the day, since healthy skunks go out only after dark.

If you suspect your dog has been bitten by a skunk, be extremely careful. Even though your dog's vaccinations will protect him, you could catch rabies if saliva in the wound penetrates a cut in your skin. Wear latex gloves when treating your dog, and call your doctor (and your veterinarian) immediately.

thoroughly, then rinse it off. Skunk spray is extremely potent, Dr. Gluckman adds, so you may need to repeat the peroxide baths several times before the stench wanes. Don't let him dry off. Just rinse him thoroughly, then wash and repeat until the smell is under control.

Bring out the tomato juice. "Hunters with dogs that routinely get skunked often wash them with tomato juice," says Kenneth Harkin, D.V.M., assistant professor in the Department of Clinical Sciences at Kansas State University's College of Veterinary Medicine in Manhattan. "Your dog will smell a little like a pizza when you're done, but it beats the skunk smell." After

washing him with his regular shampoo and rinsing him well, pour tomato juice over him and work it into his coat thoroughly. Let the tomato juice soak in for 10 to 20 minutes, then rinse him well and shampoo again. The combination of the tomato juice and shampoo will go a long way toward taming the skunk smell, says Dr. Harkin. However, tomato juice can stain light-colored fur pink.

Give him a club soda. Groomers have found club soda a helpful remedy, says Gabriel. It is preferable to use it at room temperature or to warm it slightly. Apply the soda to your dog's coat, letting it soak in. Follow up by washing him with his regular shampoo.

FAST FIX Many groomers swear that Massengill, a medicated douche, is great for reducing the stench of skunk spray. For a medium-sized dog, mix two ounces of Massengill in a gallon of water. Pour it over your dog and leave it on for 15 minutes. Rinse him well and use his regular shampoo.

Be prepared. Pack a commercial skunk deodorizer when you take your dog hiking or camping. Products such as Skunk-Off won't eliminate skunk smell, but they reduce the odor until you get home and do a more intensive deodorizing, says Dr. Kaddatz.

Commercial skunk deodorizers are at their most effective if you shampoo your dog before using the deodorizer, advises Gabriel.

Mask the smell. Vanilla extract applied to your pet's coat with a cloth won't eliminate the smell of skunk spray, but it will make your pet a little less smelly while the odor wears off.

Sunburn

When the sun's packing a punch, dogs need sunscreen and shelter in the shade every bit as much as humans. Too much sun can lead to sunburn, long-term skin damage, or, in extreme cases, skin cancer.

"Most dogs aren't very susceptible to sunburn as long as their time outside isn't excessive," says Thomas Lewis, D.V.M., a veterinarian in private practice in Mesa, Arizona. "But you do need to be careful with light-skinned dogs, such as bull terriers, Dalmatians or Samoyeds."

Even though your dog's coat provides some protection from the sun—dogs with long, dense coats are better protected than those with short coats—the belly, tips of the ears, and bridge of the nose have little or no fur. Not surprisingly, these are the spots most vulnerable to sunburn.

To ease the sting of sunburn and prevent it in the future, here's what you can do.

FAST FIX. One of the quickest ways to ease the pain of sunburn is to spray the area with a mist of witch hazel. Witch hazel has numbing properties and evaporates very quickly, making the area feel cool and comfortable, says Daryl B. Leu, D.V.M., a veterinarian in private practice in Portland, Oregon. Repeat the treatment every few hours.

Apply a cold compress. The heat from sunburn can penetrate through several layers of skin. To provide deep cooling, wet a washcloth or a small towel with cool water, wring it out, and place it on the sunburned area for a few minutes, or until it gets warm. Then rewet the cloth and apply it again, repeating the process several times.

Give a soothing soak. For sunburns on the belly, a cool bath is one of the easiest ways to take away the heat. "Adding a little colloidal oatmeal is even better, because it will soothe the irritation and itch, making your dog less likely to scratch an already tender area," says Daryl B. Leu, D.V.M., a veterinarian in private practice in

A misting with witch hazel works like a charm to relieve the sting of sunburn on this Staffordshire bull terrier-mix.

Portland, Oregon. Put a few inches of cool water in the tub and add a little colloidal oatmeal to the water.

Some dogs will happily lie down in water, but others will take a little persuading. Once he's lying down, just let him relax for a few minutes. Don't use shampoo, however, because it can dry the skin, making it even more irritated. "If your dog is really uncomfortable, give him an oatmeal bath several times a day," advises Dr. Leu. Otherwise, soak him once a day until the dead skin sloughs off.

Put back the moisture. Sunburned skin is dry skin in need of a "drink," says Dr. Lewis. The juice from an aloe vera plant is a great moisturizer, and it also helps burned skin heal more quickly. If you have an aloe vera plant at home, break a segment of the plant in half, which will release the soothing gel. You can also buy aloe vera lotions and creams at pharmacies. Apply the aloe vera once or twice a day until the skin is looking healthy again.

Use an anesthetic spray. Over-the-counter anesthetic sprays, such as Solarcaine and Lanacaine will quickly numb the pain of sunburn. "You want to keep your dog from scratching his irritated skin, which could lead to infection," says Dr. Leu. "Topical anesthestics do a good job of cooling and protecting the skin." You can also use an anesthetic ointment. They don't contain alcohol as the sprays do, making them a little more comfortable to use. Apply an anesthetic for the first day or so, when the sunburn is most painful.

Use vitamin E. Burnt noses need special attention because they're more prone to scarring after sunburn than other body parts, says Dr. Lewis. The gel from a vitamin E capsule will relieve the pain and also help prevent scarring. Many dogs will lick off the gel, so you may have to apply it several times, he adds.

A Nose for Trouble

Collies, Shetland sheepdogs, and other dogs with little or no pigment in their noses are prone to a condition called, aptly, collie nose. Without pigment, the nose is very sensitive to sunlight, which can lead to painful burns. Some owners permanently tattoo these dogs' noses black, but it won't protect them from the sun, says Daryl B. Leu, D.V.M., a veterinarian with a dermatology referral practice in Portland, Oregon. Wearing sunscreen and staying out of bright sun is the only way to keep their noses healthy.

The puppy with the blue merle coloring (center) has the poorest nose pigmentation of these three Australian shepherd puppies. He'll need plenty of protection from the sun.

Do dogs need eye protection?

Though he'd look cool in a pair of shades, does your dog really need to have his eyes protected from the sun's glare? "Some dogs do seem very squinty in the sun," says Ken Abrams, D.V.M,. a veterinary ophthalmologist in private practice in Warwick, Rhode Island.

"If a dog is very sensitive to the sun, he could be fitted with tinted lenses without any vision correction, but it would be an expensive process," says Dr. Abrams. "I recently fitted a tinted lens for a movie star dog with a large pupil resulting from a previous eye problem and surgery. But if your dog is squinty, it's probably best just to keep him in the shade and spare him the surgery."

A much easier strategy than surgery is to fit your dog with a sun visor, which is available from pet supply stores.

Time your outings. The sun in the summer months is usually at its most intense between 10:00 a.m. and 4:00 p.m. If your dog is prone to sunburn, it's a good idea to keep him inside during these times, says Dr. Leu, and to take your walks either in the morning or evening hours. This is especially important if you live at a high altitude, where the sun's burning rays are more intense.

Put on some sunscreen. An easy way to prevent sunburn (and skin cancer) is to slather your dog's ears, nose, and belly with sunscreen. "Use a sunscreen with an SPF (sun protection factor) of 15 or above," says Dr. Lewis. "Human sunscreens are fine, but avoid those that contain zinc oxide or PABA. Both these ingredients can be dangerous should your dog decide to lick the sunscreen off."

Protect him with shade. Shaded areas in the yard will give your dog welcome protection from the glare of the sun. These can be as simple as a lean-to or a leafy tree, or as luxurious as a beach umbrella. On outdoor outings, take an umbrella along with you, and make sure your dog actually uses it. Dogs can't be expected to know when they are getting burned—they will play in the sun for hours unless you encourage them to take a break.

Try some headgear. Pet supply stores sell a variety of caps equipped with sun-shades, which will help protect the ears and nose. "I've seen a number of dogs wearing sunbonnets or caps," says Dr. Leu. If they will tolerate this fashion statement, it's worth a try, he says.

Slip on a shirt. Putting a T-shirt on your pet is an easy way to minimize harmful rays damaging his skin. The basic cotton T-shirt has an SPF of only about seven, so do this in conjunction with sunscreen.

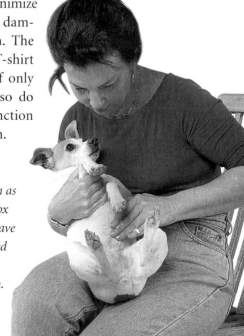

Dogs with short white coats, such as this miniature fox terrier, should have sunscreen applied to the belly to prevent sunburn.

Ticks

It's bad enough that ticks live on blood, sometimes feeding for days and swelling up to 50 times their pre-meal size. But these little bloodsuckers are more than unpleasant. They can also transmit serious diseases like Lyme disease, Rocky Mountain spotted fever, and encephalitis. In rare cases, they can even cause a type of paralysis in which a pet's hindquarters, and in some cases the entire body, becomes progressively weaker.

There are more than 1,000 species of tick. They don't all cause disease, but they all share a penchant for blood. Since there's no easy way to tell which ticks are safe and which are worrisome, it's essential to get them off your dog as soon as possible, says Jody Sandler, D.V.M., director of veterinary services for Guiding Eyes for the Blind in Yorktown Heights, New York. "A tick has to be on your dog for 48 to 72 hours in order to transmit disease," he adds. "This gives you a good amount of time to remove it."

A tick isn't always eager to let go, however. It feeds by burrowing its head beneath the skin, latching on with a dartlike anchor underneath its mouth. The anchor has small teeth that curve backward, which is what makes ticks so hard to remove. It doesn't take a lot of finesse to pull them loose, but it does take some strength. Here's what you need to do.

- Immobilize the tick by dabbing it with rubbing alcohol, says Lowell Ackerman, D.V.M., Ph.D., a veterinary dermatologist in private

REMOVING TICKS SAFELY

If you find a tick on your dog, remove it as soon as possible. Dab the area with rubbing alcohol, then grasp the tick as close to your dog's skin as possible with tweezers. Gently, but firmly, pull the tick out. Try not to squeeze while pulling, and be careful not to break off the body, leaving the head in the skin. Swab the area with antiseptic solution. If your dog shows any signs of paralysis, consult your veterinarian at once.

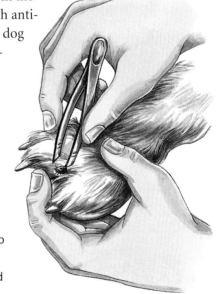

Using the tweezers, grasp the tick right up against the skin, so that the head isn't left behind.

practice in Mesa, Arizona, and author of *Skin and Haircoat Problems in Dogs*. "This sort of anesthetizes the tick, relaxing it so it can be removed more easily."

- Don't waste time putting gasoline or kerosene on a tick, and you definitely don't want to burn it with the end of a match. "These strategies don't work and they could hurt your dog," says Dr. Ackerman.

- Grasp the tick firmly with a pair of tweezers, getting as close to the head as possible. Pull slowly and steadily on the tweezers. Within five to 10 seconds you should feel the tick loosening its grip. By pulling slowly rather than jerking, the entire head will come out along with the body. Pulling too quickly, on the other hand, often causes the head to remain embedded in the skin. "The head itself is not infectious, and the normal growth of the skin will push it out in a few days," Dr. Sandler adds.

- Try not to touch a tick with your bare hands. "If you happen to have a small cut on your finger, you could contract anything the tick might be carrying," warns Dr. Ackerman. If you don't have tweezers and must use your fingers to remove a tick, he recommends putting some plastic wrap over your fingers, which essentially creates a thin glove.

- After removing the tick, dab the area with a topical antiseptic, such as Betadine solution. Then get rid of the tick—either by flushing it down the toilet or by dropping it in a jar of rubbing alcohol or insecticide. You may want to preserve one in alcohol so that your vet or doctor can tell you if it's the kind of tick that carries any diseases that may be a threat to dogs in certain regions of the country.

Preventing Problems

Ticks thrive in many parts of the country, and it's almost impossible to avoid them. If your dog spends any time outdoors, sooner or later she's going to come home with an unwanted hitchhiker or two. To get rid of ticks before they latch on, here's what veterinarians advise.

Check her often. Unlike fleas, which hop around so fast you can hardly see them, ticks stay in one place, which makes them easier to spot. Dr. Sandler recommends checking for ticks often, especially when your dog has been playing in brush or tall grass.

Ticks will latch on anywhere on the body, but they're especially fond of lightly furred areas—around the ears, for example, or on the

This golden retriever is groomed daily for ticks, with special attention given to lightly furred areas, such as around the ears, the belly, and the legs.

legs, between the toes, or on the belly. Even though adult ticks are fairly easy to spot—and feel—younger ticks (called nymphs) aren't much bigger than poppy seeds. The easiest way to spot the younger ticks is to go through your dog's hair with a fine-toothed comb, looking for little black dots next to the skin, says Dr. Sandler. If you find any unattached ticks on your dog's hair, comb them out with a fine-toothed comb and drop them into rubbing alcohol or insecticide.

Try a combination approach. A popular flea medication called Frontline, applied to a dog's back, also works against ticks, says Dr. Ackerman. Even when a tick manages to attach, the active ingredient in Frontline will cause it to release its grip within 24 hours, before it has time to spread disease. Applying Frontline once a month will give good protection against both fleas and ticks, he says.

Keep her in a sunny spot. Dogs often enjoying napping in shady patches in the yard. Unfortunately, they may have plenty of company. "Ticks aren't sun worshippers," explains Laurel Kaddatz, D.V.M., a veterinarian in private practice in Fairport, New York. "They go for cool, overgrown places, in shrubbery or tall grasses lining a yard." Although playing out in direct sun isn't advisable for your dog, those areas that get some full sun during the day are where you want her to stay even after the sun has moved on, says Dr. Kaddatz. "Your dog is less likely to pick up a tick there than in the underbrush."

Keep up with lawn care. Grass that's mowed often traps less moisture and gets much more sun, which will help keep ticks under control. Don't forget to trim long grass near trees and fences, which often escapes the mower's blades. "Don't put out the welcome mat for ticks," says Dr. Ackerman. "Clear away all of your underbrush."

Get rid of rodents. Young ticks initially bite rodents before making the transition to dogs. Keeping your yard rodent-free will also help in the battle against ticks. Control rodents by removing rocks, brush, woodpiles, or other debris that provides places for them to hide. Also, move bird feeders away from the house because the seeds may attract rodents along with the birds.

Take care on outings. When you're taking your dog hiking, protect her with a flea and tick spray containing pyrethrins, recommends Dr. Sandler. "Or spray her within a minute of your return, and then check her over," he adds.

Protect her with a collar. Try a tick collar containing an active ingredient called amitraz, which repels ticks. "You can use these collars in conjunction with other tick-control methods," explains Dr. Ackerman. And these collars are safe around kids, unlike some combination flea-and-tick collars, he says.

A protective spray will discourage ticks from hitching a ride on this black Labrador-mix.

Urinary Tract Problems

If your dog is begging to be let out all the time, be patient. She probably has a urinary tract infection. This makes it nearly impossible for dogs to "hold it" for long periods of time. Although any dog can get a urinary tract infection, they're more common in females because their shorter urethras (the tube that carries urine from the bladder) make it easier for bacteria to travel upward into the bladder. Males, with their extra inches of anatomy, are less likely to be affected, explains Rance Sellon, D.V.M., assistant professor in the Department of Clinical Sciences at Washington State University in Pullman.

Urinary tract infections are almost always treated with antibiotics and can be quite serious if not treated promptly, says Shelly Vaden, D.V.M., associate professor of internal medicine at the College of Veterinary Medicine at North Carolina State University in Raleigh. Symptoms to watch out for include:

- **Straining to urinate.** Dogs with urinary tract infections often have the urge to urinate even when the bladder's almost empty. They'll take longer than usual and will strain to make things happen—often without results.
- **Painful urination.** An infection can make the inside of the urethra raw and irritated, says Dr. Sellon. "Dogs will experience a burning sensation while urinating," she says. They'll often lick their genitals when they're done—their way of easing the sting.
- **Dark or bloody urine.** Dogs with urinary tract infections frequently have blood in the urine, which can turn it red or rust-colored. (Check the color by getting your dog to urinate on a newspaper or a piece of cloth.) The urine often has an unusually foul or strong odor.

Keep Her Comfortable

If caught early, most urinary tract infections are easy to treat with medications, although it may take a week or more before your dog is fully recovered. To keep her comfortable in the meantime, here's what veterinarians recommend.

Provide frequent toilet breaks. It's important to let her out as often as she needs to go, even if this means having a neighbor drop by if you're going to be away for more than a few hours. Not only will this keep her more comfortable, it will also help to rid the bladder of bacteria that may cause further problems.

Explore the neighborhood. Take your dog for extra walks when she has a urinary tract infection and encourage her to urinate often. This will help flush more bacteria from the bladder.

Give her citrus juice. Citrus juices make urine more acidic, which helps to reduce the number of bacteria in the urine and also eases painful urination. Mix an ounce or two of juice with her breakfast for two or three days if she won't drink it straight.

Pour more water. Encourage your dog to drink water so she'll urinate more often. This will help wash away bacteria before they do harm. She doesn't need a large volume of water—little and often is best.

Vomiting

Most dogs, sooner or later, will gulp down something better left alone, such as garbage, dirty water, or a baby's toy. Fortunately, their digestive system knows what should get the green light and what should be tossed back. "Dogs have a very good and very active reflex to throw up," says Brad Fenwick, D.V.M., of Kansas State University's College of Veterinary Medicine in Manhattan. "This serves them very well in eliminating bad stuff from their systems."

Vomiting isn't only a dog's way of giving a bad restaurant review. They will also vomit when they eat too fast, get overly excited, or get a little carsick. A sudden change in diet is another common cause of vomiting.

Even if your dog looks as hungry as this Border collie, it is best not to feed him for 24 hours after he's vomited. Otherwise he may well vomit again—and he won't thank you for that.

Most dogs will vomit once or twice and then go about their business without any problems. Even if your dog has a mild case of food poisoning, he'll probably be fine within a day. To keep his stomach calm in the meantime—and to prevent additional messes in the future—here's what vets recommend.

Put him on a fast. Keep food out of your dog's stomach for at least 24 hours after he's been sick, says Stuart Gluckman, D.V.M., a veterinarian in private practice in Mendon, New York. If there's nothing going into your dog's stomach, nothing will come out, and he'll recover a little more quickly, he explains.

LET'S TRY THAT AGAIN

Dogs throw back their food in two ways—they vomit, and they regurgitate. When vomiting, they put in a lot of abdominal effort and heaving. With regurgitation, they simply pitch back on the floor what they just ate—no heaving, no abdominal effort. "Regurgitation is a normal, biological behavior in dogs," explains Kenneth Harkin, D.V.M., assistant professor in the Department of Clinical Sciences at Kansas State University's College of Veterinary Medicine in Manhattan. "You will often see a pattern of eat-regurgitate-re-eat. It may seem awfully gross to us, but most often on that second time down, the food stays down," he explains.

Resume giving food gradually. When your dog is feeling a little better, give him small amounts of food every four hours, says Dr. Gluckman. Bland items are best, like boiled, unsalted, unflavored white rice. If the rice stays down, you can then offer tiny bits of boiled skinless chicken. You should gradually work up to feeding your dog normally again over a period of three to seven days.

Ration his water. Dogs often get very thirsty when they've been vomiting. Unfortunately, the extra water can make them sick all over again. "Once the vomiting has subsided for three to four hours, give him room-temperature water in very small amounts every two to three hours," says Dr. Gluckman.

Coat his stomach. An easy way to stop queasiness is to give him an over-the-counter stomach-soother, such as Kaopectate (one teaspoon for each 10 pounds of body weight, every four hours), or Pepto-Bismol (one teaspoon for each 20 pounds of body weight, every four to six hours). Check with your vet as dosages can vary.

Slow him down. Dogs that are very fast eaters are prone to vomiting because they gulp large amounts of air—and this can propel the food right back up again. One way to slow them down is to place a large rock or some other object in

CALL FOR HELP

Dogs are pretty indiscriminate about what they eat. They'll swallow poison as readily as tasty scraps, and they don't think twice about swallowing objects that could block their esophagus or small intestine.

"If your dog repeatedly attempts to vomit and nothing emerges, he could have an item such as a bone, a small ball, or a piece of carpet stuck in his esophagus," says Kenneth Harkin, D.V.M., assistant professor in the Department of Clinical Sciences at Kansas State University's College of Veterinary Medicine in Manhattan.

Vomiting that won't quit can also be a sign of poisoning, says Dr. Harkin. It's particularly worrisome when there's blood in the vomit because this could possibly mean your dog has damaged his insides.

Vomiting that won't quit is always a sign of problems, says Dr. Harkin. If it goes on for more than a few minutes, or if your dog has other symptoms, such as a fever or lethargy, get him to a veterinarian right away.

Food spread out on a cookie sheet takes longer to eat, so your dog won't gulp in as much air.

the food bowl. (Choose an object that's too big to swallow.) They will be forced to work a little harder to get their food and won't get the chance to gulp. Or you can spread your dog's food out on a cookie sheet. He will have to take his time over it and won't be able to swallow all the food in a few giant mouthfuls along with large amounts of air.

Worms

Dogs are fun-loving creatures that get a kick out of romping in the park and playing with other dogs. But while they're catching up on their social lives, they could also be catching something a lot less fun.

Worms are easily passed from dog to dog and, in some cases, from dogs to people, explains Robert Ridley, D.V.M., Ph.D., professor of pathology at Kansas State University's College of Veterinary Medicine in Manhattan. Dogs also catch worms from fleas or from walking in areas where worms thrive, such as public parks. Virtually all puppies are born with worms—or get them soon after birth—and most adult dogs will get them at some time in their lives.

It certainly isn't pleasant to discover worms in your dog's stool, but in most cases these worms don't cause anything worse than a little diarrhea. The worms you can't see, however, like

CALL FOR HELP

Even though worms usually aren't a serious health threat, they often multiply to huge numbers in the body. Some dogs can harbor thousands of worms at one time, which may cause them to lose large amounts of blood and nutrients. Besides causing diarrhea and vomiting, worms can be itchy, and infected dogs will often scoot on their bottoms to get relief. Blood in the stools may be a sign of whipworms, while tarry-looking stools can indicate a hookworm infestation. "Tarry or jet black stools may mean intestinal bleeding. This is serious and needs veterinary help," says Stuart Gluckman, D.V.M., a veterinarian in private practice in Mendon, New York.

Parasitic worms are prodigious breeders—each tapeworm segment, for example, contains thousands of eggs.

Tapeworm

Whipworms

Roundworms

whipworms or hookworms, can cause diarrhea, weight loss, weakness, anemia, and nutritional deficiencies. They can also put a strain on your dog's immune system, Dr. Ridley explains. And any kind of worm, if it multiplies long enough in the body, can make your dog ill.

Even though you can buy worming medications in pet supply stores, these work only against certain types of worm and may not be strong enough to be effective against all infestations. You'll need to ask your vet which treatment is best. In addition, there are some things you can do to relieve the symptoms and help prevent your dog getting reinfected.

These cocker spaniel puppies are checked regularly for worms, which can be caught from eggs in the dirt.

Check for problems. It's worth taking a close look at your dog's stools every other day or so. Even though some worms are invisible, the most common culprits, tapeworms, can be seen in the stool and resemble short grains of white rice. You'll also see them on the skin and fur around the anus, Dr. Ridley adds. It's a lot easier—and much healthier—to treat worms early on before they have a chance to get established. Since some of the most troublesome worms can be seen only with a microscope, it's worth taking a stool sample to your vet once a year.

Keep the yard clean. Worm eggs such as hookworms, roundworms, and whipworms travel out of the body in the stool. "They can contaminate the yard and soil for a long time," says Stuart Gluckman, D.V.M., a veterinarian in private practice in Mendon, New York. "In freezing weather, the eggs simply lie dormant, then incubate and hatch in the warm weather." It's not unusual for dogs to get worms just from walking through a park or lying in the dirt. They also get infected by licking their feet, which may harbor microscopic eggs. "If everyone picked up after their dogs, we wouldn't have such a worm problem," says Dr. Ridley.

Get rid of fleas. Fleas do a lot more than cause a little itching. They also carry tapeworms, and dogs can get infected when they inadvertently swallow fleas during their usual grooming. Getting rid of his fleas will help prevent tapeworms. For more information see page 61.

Clean up after visitors. No matter how conscientious you are about cleaning up after your dog, other owners may not be as dedicated. It's worth patrolling your yard every day to see if other dogs have left their calling cards. This is probably the best way to keep worms at bay.

Stop the chase. Many dogs have a keen hunting instinct and fleet feet to go along with it. Unfortunately, dogs often get tapeworms from eating rabbits, mice, or other rodents, says Dr. Ridley. Even if you live in a rural area without busy roads, keeping him on a leash will reduce the risk when he roams. Have him tested for worms several times a year instead of annually if he literally catches his dinner on the run.

Calm his stomach. Deworming medications work rapidly and you'll see results right away. However, some dogs with worms will have a little diarrhea or vomiting. A quick way to calm their stomachs and make stools firmer is with Kaopectate, an over-the-counter medication, says Dr. Gluckman. "Kaopectate is safe to use, but if symptoms persist for more than 24 hours after deworming, contact your veterinarian," he says. Give one teaspoon of Kaopectate for every 10 pounds of your dog's body weight.

PART THREE

GIVING LONG-TERM CARE

Dogs are remarkably resilient, but even the healthiest dog
will occasionally need long-term help—for example, when arthritis
doesn't go away. Most conditions can be treated at home with lifestyle changes,
like altering diets or going for more walks. And by working closely with your
veterinarian, you'll be able to ensure that your dog has the best life possible,
no matter what her age or stage of life.

Aging

Dogs do everything a lot faster than people do. They wake up in an instant (and go to sleep just as readily), run when walking would do, and make the transition from puppy to adult in less than a year. And of course, they age more quickly than people do.

Dogs live an average of 13 years, although the age at which your dog reaches senior status depends largely on his size. Small dogs usually age more slowly than big ones. A seven-year-old toy poodle, for example, is still in the bloom of middle age, while a seven-year-old Great Dane is an elder statesman.

As dogs get older they often experience many of the same changes people do, like joint pain, weight gain, or a dip in energy. But even though you can't stop time, there's no reason older dogs should be any less enthusiastic and healthy than their younger friends. Essentially, your dog is as old as he feels. By not coddling your dog when he becomes a senior citizen, you can help him feel like a puppy. "Exercise plays a huge part in

staying young," says Susan G. Wynn, D.V.M., a veterinarian in private practice in Marietta, Georgia. "If your dog is young or middle-aged, exercise will help him age more gracefully. Older dogs also age better with consistent exercise."

By paying attention to your dog's exercise habits and diet, and being attentive to changes in his health, you can have a dramatic impact on how he feels and ages. Veterinarians have discovered some simple, practical ways that will essentially roll back time, allowing older dogs to feel much younger than their years. Here's what they recommend.

Keep him moving. Regular exercise will maintain your dog's all-important muscle mass, as well as helping with weight control and blood circulation. Also, exercise is good if he's becoming constipated, which can sometimes happen when dogs start to slow down. Take your dog for a couple of half-hour walks a day, advises Robert Flecker, D.V.M., a veterinarian in private practice in Tualatin, Oregon. Keep the pace moderate. Don't let him break into a sprint if one day he feels more athletic than usual. "Dogs don't know their limits," says Jan Wolf, D.V.M., a veterinarian in private practice in Kenosha, Wisconsin, "so it's important to use sound judgment." Talk to your vet about the right level of exercise for your dog, then be consistent with the exercise regimen.

Feed him normally. If your dog is doing well on the food he's always eaten, don't switch him to a senior diet just because he's getting on in years, says Dr. Wynn. A low-fat senior diet

This longhaired dachshund-mix is an elderly dog who is enthusiastic about life. His owner watches carefully for weight problems, which dachshunds are susceptible to as they get older.

Elderly dogs, such as this Dalmatian, need to keep up their gentle daily exercise. Walking not only keeps the joints working, it also helps avoid constipation.

fish oil supplements can make your dog feel years younger, says Dr. Wynn. There's scientific evidence that salmon oil can slow kidney damage in dogs, and it may help with autoimmune problems, heart disease, and skin disease. "When we put older dogs on an antioxidant blend and fish oil, the owners say they get around better, are brighter, and just seem to feel better," says Dr. Wynn. Use these supplements under your veterinarian's guidance, and use only veterinary formulations of antioxidant blends—those designed for human have a different balance of ingredients, she cautions.

Join the weight-watchers. Older dogs tend to put on weight as their metabolism slows and creakiness sets in. But excess weight puts added pressure on sore joints and backs, says Dr. Wynn. Forgo weight-reducing or senior diets, which may not have enough high-quality meat ingredients. Instead, give your dog slightly smaller servings of a high-quality food. Supplement the diet with fresh vegetables. Pretty soon you'll have a thinner—and healthier—pooch.

Stop the handouts. Resist the temptation to slip your dog table scraps. They won't help his weight, and his tummy will take even less kindly to rich food than it did when he was younger. "Even a tiny piece of Easter ham is a tough thing for an older dog to handle," says Dr. Wolf.

Tantalize his taste buds. Loss of appetite can be a sign of illness in any dog, young or old. But if your older pet has a clean bill of health and still doesn't go for his food, it might be that his sense of smell has diminished. You can make mealtimes more drool-worthy by adding some smelly, low-fat additions to his food, like tuna oil or clam juice, suggests Dr. Wynn. Or try

can actually be detrimental. Low-fat diets, which usually rely on grains as the main protein source, tend also to be low in protein. This can be a problem, says Dr. Wynn, because extra protein may be needed by older dogs to repair damaged tissue. Moreover, if your dog gets used to a low-fat diet, he might be unable to handle higher fat levels. Exposure to extra fat could lead to pancreatitis, a serious illness in dogs.

Try some supplements. A blend of antioxidants (containing Vitamins A, C and E, as well as beta carotene and selenium) coupled with

heating some canned food in the microwave to warm it up and bring out the aroma, then serve it with his regular meal.

Get out the toothbrush. Keeping your dog's teeth clean and healthy is important at any age, but it's vital in an older pet. If an older dog's teeth haven't been well cared for his entire life, he may be looking at tooth loss—or worse. His mouth is the gateway to the rest of his body, and the bacteria introduced to his body through tooth and gum decay can lead to heart, liver, and kidney problems. Decay can also make it painful for him to eat. Your veterinarian can give his teeth a thorough cleaning. After that, keep them clean by giving them a really good, but gentle scrub every day with a small dog toothbrush. Smear the brush with a little pet toothpaste, available in pet supply stores.

Help stop itching. Older dogs, particularly those who had skin problems when they were younger, tend to have dry, flaky skin. You can help stop your dog from itching by giving him a nutritional supplement containing skin-healthy oils. Choose one like Derm Caps, which is available from your veterinarian, suggests Dr. Wolf.

Stay in close contact with your vet. "It really helps to have a close relationship with your vet when your dog is getting on in years," says Dr. Flecker. A thorough physical exam and routine annual blood tests will give your vet the chance to identify diseases, like kidney or liver problems, before your dog is even showing any symptoms.

CALL FOR HELP

Changes are natural in older dogs, but don't assume every change is caused by old age. Your dog could be suffering from something that's easily treated. With proper care there's a good chance he'll soon be feeling fine.

There are a number of symptoms you need to watch out for, says Susan G. Wynn, D.V.M., a veterinarian in private practice in Marietta, Georgia. They are:

- Loss of energy or appetite
- Increased water consumption
- Increased urination
- Discharges
- Sores that don't heal
- Changes in weight
- Abnormal odors
- Lumps or bumps on the skin
- Color changes in the skin or eyes
- Coughing or sneezing

With early detection your veterinarian has a much better chance of helping you manage, and in some cases cure, your dog's health problems.

This Labrador-mix enjoys retiring to his clean and comfortable bed. The soft surface also helps keep his joints loose and limber.

Arthritis

It would be nice if dogs stayed loose and limber all their lives. But dogs, like people, tend to get a little stiff and creaky as they get older, usually because of arthritis—a painful condition that occurs when cartilage in the joints starts breaking down. There are several forms of arthritis, but the most common is osteoarthritis, also known as "wear-and-tear" arthritis. "Just as eyes and skin deteriorate with age, so does cartilage," explains William Fortney, D.V.M., a veterinarian in the Department of Clinical Sciences at Kansas State University's College of Veterinary Medicine in Manhattan.

Younger dogs occasionally get arthritis—because of injuries or infections, for example, or because they have conditions such as hip dysplasia, in which joints simply aren't put together the way they should be. Most of the time, however, arthritis is an older dog's condition.

Arthritis is potentially serious, and dogs with this condition always need to be under a veterinarian's care. But in most cases you can control or even eliminate pain and stiffness with simple home remedies. In addition, there are many ways to protect the joints while your dog's still young, so arthritis never becomes an issue.

Rub away stiffness. Massaging your dog's hips, elbows, back, neck, and knees for a few minutes every day will help improve blood flow and keep the muscles and joints much looser, says Patrick Tate, D.V.M., a veterinarian in private practice in St. Louis, Missouri. Massage doesn't have to be fancy, he adds. Just apply gentle, deep pressure with your fingertips to the areas surrounding the joints. While you're at it, gently move the legs through their full range of motion. These daily "warm-ups" will not only help prevent arthritis pain, but will provide quick relief once it begins.

Keep him active. During arthritis flare-ups, most dogs will prefer lying on the carpet to running around the yard. But regular exercise is essential because it causes the body to secrete lubricating fluid into the joints, so they move more smoothly. Exercise also strengthens the muscles surrounding their joints, which helps prevent arthritis from getting worse, says Dr. Fortney. Walking is one of the best forms of exercise because it puts relatively little pressure on the painful joints. Even when your dog is hurting, take him out several times a day for short,

A daily massage greatly eases the soreness and stiffness of this poodle-mix's arthritic joints.

Because swimming is a nonweight-bearing exercise, this golden retriever can thoroughly enjoy himself without putting pressure on sore, arthritic joints.

gentle walks. On days when he's feeling more limber, you can increase the exercise a bit. Don't overdo it, though, or he may get even more sore later on.

Head for the water. For dogs that like the water, swimming is great exercise because it moves the joints and muscles through their full range of motion, and the water dramatically reduces pressure on the joints, says Dr. Tate.

Keep an eye on his weight. Dogs that are overweight are much more likely to suffer from arthritis than their leaner friends. And for those that already have arthritis, the extra padding puts unnecessary pressure on the joints, causing them to wear more quickly, says Dr. Tate.

Apart from additional exercise, the only way to help dogs lose weight is to feed them less. Dr. Tate recommends reducing what goes in his bowl by 10 to 20 percent. If he hasn't lost any weight in two to three weeks, it's fine to reduce

the food a little more. If he still is looking a bit portly, you'll need to talk to your vet about starting a more rigorous weight-loss plan.

It's not only what goes in the food bowl that causes weight gain. Most of us give our dogs a lot of treats—everything from dog biscuits to tasty leftovers—and these extra calories can quickly add up. You don't have to quit pampering your dog, but you will want to reduce the "extras." One way to do this is to give him a quarter of a biscuit instead of a whole one. Or try replacing the treats altogether with low-cal, healthful snacks, like raw carrots.

Give him a comfy place to sleep. All dogs enjoy a comfortable place to sleep, but for dogs with arthritis it's a necessity, says Karen Mateyak, D.V.M., a veterinarian in private practice in Brooklyn, New York. She recommends getting your dog an orthopedic bed made with egg-crate foam, which is available from pet-supply stores and catalogs. And since arthritis gets worse when it's cold, put it in a cosy, warm, draft-free place.

Bundle him up. Your dog's thick fur coat does a great job keeping him warm. But when his joints are hurting during flare-ups and there's a real nip in the air, you may want to slip

This Maltese-mix's joints don't ache as much when he enjoys the warmth of his winter coat.

him into a sweater or coat made for dogs, says Dr. Mateyak. This will provide a little extra warmth and insulation, which will help keep the joints loose and limber.

Raise his bowl. Dogs won't let a little bit of arthritis get in the way of supper time, but in some cases bending down to eat can trigger pain and stiffness in the neck. Some dogs, in fact, are simply too stiff to reach their bowls. To make mealtimes more comfortable, you may want to raise food and water bowls off the floor—by putting them on a low chair, for example. Or you can buy special elevated food stands that are made for dogs with arthritis.

Give him a helping hand. The frustrating thing about arthritis is that even when the pain goes away for a while, it invariably comes back. One of the best ways to keep your dog more comfortable during flare-ups is to look for ways to help him get around—by putting a ramp next to stairs, for example, or lifting him up when he's trying to stand in the morning.

Give over-the-counter relief. Veterinarians often recommend treating arthritis pain with buffered aspirin, such as Ascriptin, says Dr. Mateyak. The usual dose is one-quarter of a 325-milligram tablet for every 10 pounds of weight, given twice a day. Check with your veterinarian before starting aspirin therapy, Dr. Mateyak says. Always give aspirin with meals and use the buffered kind because nonbuffered aspirin will be hard on his stomach.

Try an all-natural alternative. The supplement glucosomine has proven to be very helpful for arthritis, says Dr. Tate. It hasn't undergone a lot of scientific scrutiny, but it has no known side effects and it appears to regenerate the joint cartilage and relieve pain and inflammation. It's available over-the-counter in health food stores and from dog catalogs or by prescription (under the name Cosequin) from your vet. Look for the words "Glucosomine" and "Chondroitin" on the label, says Dr. Tate, and ask your vet how much to give.

Try a taste of the sea. A nutritional product made from freeze-dried perna mussel, an edible shellfish, is recommended for arthritis and may help your pet. It provides "support" to the connective tissue, says Dr. Tate. Products containing the shellfish extract, which smells like a bad day at the shore, are available at pet stores and through mail order catalogs.

FAST FIX Dogs with arthritis are usually stiffest first thing in the morning. Applying moist heat to the joints for five to 10 minutes can give instant relief.

BREED SPECIFIC

Big dogs such as Great Danes, German shepherds, Labrador retrievers, and Saint Bernards are prone to arthritis because their sheer size puts a lot of stress on the joints. These dogs also have a high risk of developing hip dysplasia, an inherited condition in which the hip joints are poorly formed, causing the cartilage to break down.

Small dogs can also get arthritis. For example, Yorkshire terriers, toy poodles, and Pomeranians tend to have "trick" knees, which can lead to arthritis later on.

Bladder Control Problems

Dogs are intelligent animals and they learn early in life that they're supposed to urinate outside and not in the house. As they get older, though, the sphincter—the muscle that controls the flow of urine—may lose some of its holding power. Without that "grip," even the most fastidious dog will start to urinate in the house and in her bed.

Incontinence occurs most often in female dogs that have been spayed, explains Patrick Tate, D.V.M., a veterinarian in private practice in St. Louis, Missouri. Low estrogen levels in female dogs might contribute in some way to incontinence, Male dogs may become incontinent as well, especially in the elderly years. Veterinarians may prescribe medications that help restore urinary sphincter continence.

Loss of bladder control can also be caused by urinary tract infections, which cause the sense of urgency, making it impossible for dogs to get outside in time, says William Fortney, D.V.M., staff veterinarian at Kansas State University's Veterinary Medicine Teaching Hospital, in Manhattan. Even though any bladder control problems should be handled by a vet, there's a lot you can do at home to keep your dog comfortable and, in some cases, prevent the problems from occurring.

For dogs with bladder control problems, doggie diapers are an effective way to keep their fur—and the carpets—dry.

BREED SPECIFIC

Any dog can get bladder problems, but they seem to be most common in Doberman pinschers, rough collies, miniature poodles, springer spaniels, old English sheepdogs, and Irish setters.

Let her out. By giving your dog the chance to go out often, there'll be less urine in her bladder, making accidents less likely, says Dr. Tate.

Dogs that are having trouble holding their urine because they're suffering from a urinary tract infection are going to need to go out a lot. Watch for the signs—waiting by the door or sniffing the carpet, for instance—that she's getting ready to go, and you'll stand a good chance of forestalling accidents. Some dogs will need to go out every couple of hours until the problem clears up, says Dr. Tate. For dogs with recurring urinary tract infections, sitting around with a full bladder only encourages harmful bacteria to thrive, Dr. Tate adds.

Encourage her to drink. Dogs prone to urinary tract infections will benefit from drinking more water, says Dr. Tate. The increase in fluids helps dilute and flush bacteria from the urinary tract. Try to get your dog to drink about one-and-a-half times her normal daily

Getting out more often gives dogs with incontinence, like this golden retriever, a lot more opportunities to urinate, so accidents at home are less likely.

water intake, he says. Dogs won't drink to order, of course, but you can help a reluctant drinker work up a thirst by adding a little salty gravy to her food or feeding her a few saltines.

Try some cranberry. Cranberry juice can acidify the urine and help stop bacteria from multiplying in the bladder, says Dr. Tate. Your dog may not be happy about drinking it, though, so you may have to try stirring it into

CALL FOR HELP

Even though bladder-control problems are fairly common, they're never normal, no matter how old your dog gets. Dogs that are urinating much more than usual—with or without proper control—may have internal problems such as diabetes, liver disease, or a hormone imbalance.

Some dogs suffer from incontinence as a result of trauma to the brain or spinal cord. When that's the cause, medicine usually does not help and your vet may recommend surgery. Surgery can also help dogs who are born with an abnormality that prevents them from holding urine properly.

"Frequent urination or increased thirst should not be ignored," says Patrick Tate, D.V.M., a veterinarian in private practice in St. Louis, Missouri. "They need to be looked at by a veterinarian."

her food. Or you can try giving her cranberry-juice capsules, available at health food stores. Check with your veterinarian for dosage.

Keep her comfortable with a waterproof bed. A pet bed specially designed to minimize the inconvenience of bed-wetting is a good option for dogs having trouble with bladder control. The beds consist of a vinyl-coated mesh fabric suspended over a removable pan. Should your dog have an accident, the fluid is drained away into the pan and she stays dry. They are available from pet supply stores and catalogs.

Fit her with a diaper. With dogs that are getting on in years, bladder-control problems are often slow to improve. To avoid accidents in the house, a simple solution is to have your dog wear diapers. Diapers specifically designed for dogs are available at pet supply stores. Or you can use a disposable baby diaper by cutting out a hole for her tail. Be sure to change diapers frequently to prevent skin irritation, says Jan Wolf, D.V.M., a veterinarian in private practice in Kenosha, Wisconsin.

121

Diabetes

We think of diabetes as a human illness, but as many as one in a hundred dogs get it too. Dogs also experience many of the same symptoms as people, such as fatigue, increased thirst, and frequent urination.

Diabetes occurs when the pancreas either produces too little insulin or the insulin it does produce doesn't work as well as it should. Insulin is a hormone that takes sugar from the blood stream and delivers it to cells throughout the body, where it's used as fuel. When the balance of insulin is right, dogs receive the necessary amount of sugar. When insulin levels fall, however, they aren't able to maintain the proper sugar balance and they get weak and tired. In addition, dogs with diabetes will burn fat to make up for the missing sugar calories, causing them to lose weight, says Robin Downing, D.V.M., a veterinarian in private practice in Windsor, Colorado.

Even though dogs with diabetes always need to be under a veterinarian's care, it's fairly easy to control the symptoms by giving twice daily injections of insulin, which replenish the body's natural supply, says Dr. Downing. In addition, there are some very effective things you can do to improve your dog's blood-sugar balance and even reduce his need for medication.

Give him high-fiber foods. One of the best ways to control diabetes is to give your dog a food that's high in fiber and low in fat, says Dr. Downing. The levels of protein should be moderate and there shouldn't be any glucose or sucrose included in the diet.

CALL FOR HELP

While giving the right amount of insulin helps control high levels of glucose in the blood stream, giving too much can make blood sugars drop to dangerous levels, causing a life-threatening condition called hypoglycemia, says Harriet Lederman, V.M.D., a veterinarian in private practice in Millburn, New Jersey. Hypoglycemia usually occurs within several hours of being given an insulin injection, she explains. Symptoms to watch for include:

- Lethargy or weakness
- Staggering and disorientation
- Seizures
- Lack of responsiveness.

Although you can treat hypoglycemia by quickly giving your dog a little honey or syrup, it's always an emergency and you need to take him to your veterinarian immediately, says Dr. Lederman.

The extra fiber slows the absorption of nutrients through the intestinal wall, so blood sugar levels don't rise too quickly after your dog eats, explains Dr. Downing. Extra fiber also helps cells make the best use of insulin, which means your dog may need a smaller dose. Lowering fat in the diet is also helpful because a low-fat diet decreases the body's need for insulin, she explains.

Dogs with diabetes are often given a prescription food. Or your veterinarian may recommend giving your dog a senior or premium weight-loss food, both of which have the right mix of fat and fiber for controlling diabetes.

It is important that your dog's diet is consistent and that it doesn't vary in quality from day to day. He must have set times for his meals. No matter how much he begs for tasty extras, it's essential to stick to the proper diet, adds Harriet Lederman, V.M.D., a veterinarian in private practice in Millburn, New Jersey. For dogs with diabetes, a rich diet can lead to pancreatic disease, she explains. "Table scraps are out."

Make some special treats. There's nothing wrong with giving your dog treats now and then, as long as you choose them carefully. The problem is that many dog biscuits and other snacks are loaded with sugar, salt, and fat, all of which can make insulin less effective.

The most healthful snacks for dogs that have diabetes are those you make yourself, says Dr.

Pomeranians are one of the breeds that has a high risk of getting diabetes.

Downing. She recommends putting some of your pet's usual chow through the food processor to make a flour. Add a little water to make a dough, then bake it until it's crunchy. Dogs love the taste, and you'll love the fact that you're giving them "extras" that will satisfy their cravings while also controlling their symptoms.

Just be sure to give your dog the treats consistently, Dr. Downing adds. Giving no treats one day and a lot the next can cause his blood-sugar levels to fluctuate, making diabetes much harder to control.

Give him more exercise. The more fit and muscular your dog is, the less insulin he'll need, says Dr. Downing. But you don't have to turn him into a canine track-and-field star to get the benefits. Even small amounts of exercise—for example, taking two, 20-minute walks every day—are helpful, as long as you are consistent.

One thing you don't want to do is let your dog laze around the house all week, then go crazy on the weekends. Long periods of inactivity followed by a sudden hard push can cause blood sugar levels to suddenly drop, a condition vets call a hypoglycemic crisis, says Dr. Downing. If you're planning an outing that will be

BREED SPECIFIC

Dogs that have a higher than usual risk of developing diabetes include dachshunds, Doberman pinschers, German shepherds, golden and Labrador retrievers, Samoyeds, Rottweilers, miniature poodles, cocker spaniels, and Pomeranians.

Diabetes hasn't slowed this German shepherd, who continues to exercise daily. Regular exercise has reduced the amount of insulin he needs.

of diluting high concentrations of glucose in the blood stream. If your dog is suddenly drinking a lot more than usual, there's a good chance he needs a change in his medication and you should call your veterinarian right away.

Encourage him to urinate more often. Dogs with diabetes naturally have a lot of sugar in the urine, which makes it easy for bacteria to flourish in the bladder and cause infections. Encouraging your dog to urinate more often will make it harder for bacteria to accumulate in the urinary tract, reducing his risk of infections.

Signs of urinary tract infections include straining to urinate, blood in the urine, or frequent licking of the genitals. If you see any of these symptoms, play it safe and call your vet right away, says Dr. Downing.

Memorize his medication. Insulin needs to be given on a regular schedule. Just to be safe, it's a good idea to memorize (and write down) the type

more vigorous than usual, make sure you bring along some extra food, she suggests. That way you'll be able to give your dog a much-needed boost before his blood sugar levels dip too far. Tell your veterinarian if your dog's exercise levels have significantly increased or decreased, Dr. Downing adds. He may need a change in the amount of insulin he's given to accommodate the change in exercise.

Watch his weight. The more weight your dog carries around, the more insulin his body needs, says Dr. Downing. She recommends weighing your dog every few weeks, and calling your vet if he seems to be gaining—or losing— weight. Luckily, the high-fiber, low-fat diet recommended for dogs with diabetes will naturally help them lose weight.

Watch how much he drinks. Dogs that are taking insulin drink normal amounts of water. Those with uncontrolled diabetes, however, will drink tremendous amounts—it's the body's way

Keep a diary listing the times when you give your dog insulin, the dosage, and any reactions he may have. This information will help your vet if there's ever a problem.

Tuesday,
4 units insulin
given before
breakfast and
dinner

Wednesday,
4 units insulin
given as above
exercised x20
minutes drinking
well

and amount of insulin he's taking, and the time you give it. If you should lose his medication—or there's an emergency and you're seeing a new veterinarian—having this information will make things a lot easier. It is also a good idea to have engraved on your dog's identification tags that he is diabetic and insulin dependent.

FAST FIX Always keep a jar of honey or Karo syrup handy. If you suspect your dog's blood sugar is dropping too low, rubbing a little honey or syrup around his mouth will provide immediate relief. Then take him to your veterinarian to make sure that he has recovered fully.

HOW TO GIVE INSULIN SHOTS

Dogs with diabetes almost always need daily insulin shots in order to stay healthy. If you've never given a shot before, the thought of needles and syringes can be a little unsettling, but it's actually easy to do.

The injections are given under the skin (not into muscles) on the scruff of the neck, where most dogs have a lot of loose skin. Make a tent of skin between your thumb and forefinger, then put the needle into the fold of skin, below your finger. It's easy to feel when the needle is through the skin and entering the empty space underneath.

"Most pets don't seem to notice the injection," says Robin Downing, D.V.M., a veterinarian in private practice in Windsor, Colorado. If you're nervous about getting started, you can practice by giving shots into an unpeeled orange, she suggests. The feel of the needle going through the orange peel is very similar to the way it feels going through the skin.

Giving shots is just one part of using insulin. It's also important to handle the medication carefully, says Dr. Downing. This means keeping it refrigerated and not shaking the bottle, she explains.

Most dogs are given the injections 30 minutes after eating, every 12 hours. But if your dog isn't eating—or he ate, but threw up—don't give insulin without calling your vet first. Giving insulin when there isn't enough food in his system can cause blood sugar levels to drop too far.

Heart Disease

Dogs don't get heart disease the way people do, which is why it's fine to give them an egg yolk now and then to keep their coats shiny. Cholesterol and saturated fat simply aren't a problem for them. But dogs may develop other kinds of heart problems, which can be quite serious if you don't take care of them right away.

In small dogs one of the heart valves may not close properly, a condition called mitral regurgitation. Large dogs are more likely to get a heart condition called dilated cardiomyopathy, in which the heart muscle enlarges and doesn't beat as vigorously as it should, says Paul D. Pion, D.V.M., a veterinary cardiologist in private practice in Sacramento, California and co-founder of the Veterinary Information Network, the largest online service for veterinarians.

In addition, some dogs develop irregular heartbeats, Dr. Pion says. These aren't always serious, but some dogs will need drugs or an artificial pacemaker to help the heart

CALL FOR HELP

Heart problems can come on fairly quickly and they're not always easy to recognize. This is a problem because dogs that develop heart disease usually need medications—in some cases, right away. The sooner you know what's going on and get your dog to the vet, the more likely he is to recover. Here's what to look for:

- He's having trouble breathing.
- He coughs, especially when he wakes up or gets excited.
- He seems lethargic or weaker than usual.
- He faints.

maintain a normal rhythm. "Pacemakers are pretty common for animals who have abnormally slow rhythms," says Dr. Pion.

Dogs with heart problems always need to be under a veterinarian's care. But in most cases there's a lot you can do to control the problem and help prevent it from getting worse. Here's what veterinarians advise.

Watch out for salt. Dogs aren't as sensitive as people to the effects of sodium, but getting too much salt in the diet can cause fluids to accumulate in the body, making the heart work harder. That's why vets usually recommend that dogs with advanced heart problems be given a low-salt diet, says Dr. Pion.

BREED SPECIFIC

About 90 percent of dogs with dilated cardiomyopathy belong to one of the following breeds: Doberman pinschers, Great Danes (right), Irish wolfhounds, Saint Bernards, cocker spaniels, golden retrievers, German shepherds, and boxers.

You can buy commercial foods that don't contain a lot of salt, but check with your vet before changing your dog's diet, Dr. Pion adds.

You may want to check with your dog, as well. Dogs, like people, often prefer salty foods and will sometimes refuse to eat when they're switched to a low-salt diet. Good nutrition is more important than worrying about salt, so if your dog doesn't seem to care for his new, low-salt food, it's better to switch back to what he's accustomed to, says Dr. Pion.

Watch his weight. One of the best things you can do to protect the heart is keep your dog trim. Dogs that are overweight have a lot more tissue than their leaner friends, and this means the heart has to pump larger amounts of blood over greater distances. Keeping him at a healthy weight reduces the workload on the heart, which helps to keep it healthy in the long run.

Get out the leash. Some people worry that exercise will be too much stress for a dog with heart disease. But there's no need to coop up your dog if he enjoys exercise. "He's a dog. Let him be a dog," advises Dr. Pion. Just be sure not to push him too hard, especially when it's hot outside.

During the summer, the best times for exercise are in the early morning and evening, when the temperatures are cooler, says Jan Wolf, D.V.M., a veterinarian in private practice in Kenosha, Wisconsin. Keep him out of direct sunlight, and keep the pace moderate.

Monitor his heart rate. Even though your vet will be listening to your dog's heart fairly often, you need to check it out for yourself once a day, says Dr. Wolf, so you are quickly aware of any changes that may need veterinary attention.

If your dog becomes exhausted after normal exercise, he may be showing the first symptoms of heart disease.

The easiest way to check the heart rate is to place your fingers on the femoral artery, found on the inside of the hind leg, running along the thigh bone about half way between the hip and the knee. Count the number of beats in 15 seconds, then multiply by four to get the number of beats per minute. Doing this regularly makes it possible to catch any changes in the heart rate so you can let your vet know what's going on.

Your vet may recommend that you keep a daily log, listing your dog's heart rate and observations about it. This allows your vet to see what has been happening in between office visits. "Getting the medication just right is a balancing act and a log can be a great help," says Dr. Pion.

Liver and Kidney Problems

Every day your dog's body produces tremendous amounts of wastes—not merely the kind you see when you're patrolling the yard with a pooper-scooper or when he stops at a fire hydrant to leave his afternoon mark, but also other byproducts of digestion and metabolism, such as mineral compounds. Many of these wastes are altered, broken down, or trapped in the kidneys and liver, which are the body's main filters. One of their key jobs is removing toxins from the blood before they accumulate in the body.

The functions of the kidneys and liver are extraordinarily complex, and it's not uncommon for them to work a little less efficiently as dogs get older. In some cases this is a normal part of the aging process. More often, kidney or liver problems occur when something—a viral or bacterial infection, for example, or exposure to harmful toxins in the environment—has caused internal damage.

The kidneys and liver are tough organs, which is why they can withstand a lifetime's exposure to harmful compounds. But this also means that they keep working even when they're damaged.

Many dogs won't show any symptoms at all until the damage is well advanced—and harder to treat, says Robin Downing, D.V.M., a veterinarian in private practice in Windsor, Colorado. The kidneys in particular have a great ability to compensate for damage—up to three-quarters of kidney function may be gone before your dog shows any sign of illness.

Dogs with advanced liver disease will usually have abdominal tenderness on the right side of their bodies. The eyes and gums may look yellow, and there may be some abdominal swelling, as well.

Dogs with advanced kidney disease will usually urinate much more than usual. The urine will be almost clear because the kidneys aren't filtering wastes the way they should, says Dr. Downing.

In addition, most dogs with advanced kidney disease will drink tremendous amounts of water. They may also have bad breath and some muscle weakness.

KIDNEY STONES

Kidney stones are relatively uncommon and usually occur in dogs as a consequence to any serious or long-term infection, damage from medication or poisons, or abnormalities in breaking down nutrients.

Diets that provide too much of certain minerals, such as calcium, can also cause kidney stones.

Symptoms may include recurrent urinary infections, blood in the urine, or pain over the back. Diagnosis is made by X-ray or ultrasound.

Treatment of kidney stones is usually strict dietary changes. In addition, some dogs will need medicine to eliminate stones and prevent them from coming back.

Hepatitis is a serious liver disease that may cause a yellow tinge in the eyes. This beagle is getting his eyes checked to make sure he's recovering properly.

The Power of Diet

Even though any kidney or liver problem is potentially serious, both organs readily respond to changes in diet. In fact, the liver has the amazing ability to regenerate damaged cells—if you act quickly, says Terry McCoy, D.V.M., a veterinarian in private practice in Corvallis, Oregon. Once the liver is given a little help, it can frequently resume its function. But it can only do this if the problem is caught early and treated early.

Dogs with liver or kidney problems always need to be under a veterinarian's care. But whether your dog is having an acute illness, like a liver or kidney infection, or he's going to need long-term care, customizing his diet is the key to keeping both of these organs healthy.

The body needs protein to regenerate cells and build tissue, in addition to running the body functions that maintain life. However, liver and kidney problems can present the challenge of balancing sufficient dietary protein intake while preventing further damage to these vital organs.

Depending on the type of liver or kidney disease diagnosed by your vet, most dogs can benefit from dietary changes. Here's what veterinarians recommend.

Keep him eating. The first priority is that your dog eats. It sounds simple, but if your veterinarian recommends a new food and your dog won't eat it, then let him have his usual diet because he will only get a lot sicker if he doesn't eat.

Give high quality protein. Many dogs with liver or kidney disease feel better when they are given a lower-than-average amount of protein that is of high quality. Some commercial foods have the proper kind of protein, or your veterinarian may recommend making home-cooked meals.

While the total protein content of the diet is a consideration, the type of protein is most important. The type of proteins found in dairy products, such as cottage cheese, are preferable to egg proteins. Proteins from soymeal and cornmeal are far less likely to cause problems than protein from meat.

Increase the fiber. Recent studies have shown that giving dogs more dietary fiber will help them cope better with liver problems.

Make dietary changes slowly. Always make changes to your dog's diet gradually—by mixing in a little of the new food with the old—

to make sure he won't rebel at the change. And don't make major changes in his diet without checking with your vet.

Feed him often. The liver does its hardest work right after meals, when huge amounts of protein, fats, and other nutrients flood the bloodstream. Giving your dog three or four small meals a day instead of one or two big ones allows the liver to work at a more leisurely pace, which will help keep him healthier.

Encourage him to drink. Dogs with kidney problems often produce tremendous amounts of urine because the kidneys aren't able to recycle fluids as well as they should. This can cause dogs to lose more fluids than they take in, which further damages the kidneys and may cause dehydration.

"Don't let the water bowl run dry," says Jan Wolf, D.V.M., a veterinarian in private practice in Kenosha, Wisconsin. In fact, you should do everything you can to encourage your dog to get more fluids into his body.

By regularly drinking plenty of water, this Labrador-mix is helping his kidneys work better.

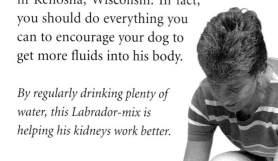

BREED SPECIFIC

Shetland sheepdogs and schnauzers are prone to liver disease, while Lhasa apsos and shih tzus may suffer from kidney problems. Bedlington terriers have a genetic tendency to get both liver and kidney diseases.

If your dog doesn't seem interested in drinking, try stirring some chicken broth into his water. Or add water or broth to his food, Dr. Wolf suggests.

Keep antifreeze locked away. One of the easiest ways to prevent kidney problems is to keep dogs away from antifreeze. Antifreeze is the number-one cause of sudden kidney failure, says Dr. Downing.

It's not enough to keep the bottle out of reach because dogs will also lap up antifreeze when it puddles under the car, adds Dr. Downing. Taking care of leaks right away will help ensure that your dog doesn't have problems later on.

Take advantage of yearly checkups. Even though it can take years before kidney or liver problems cause obvious symptoms, your veterinarian can spot problems right away during annual checkups.

"There is a golden window of opportunity where we can pick up on problems early, simply through blood and urine tests," says Dr. Downing

Overweight

It's only natural to indulge the dog you love with the occasional treat, but it's all too easy to overdose on kindness, which is why about 40 percent of American dogs are overweight. All those extra pounds can take a serious toll. Dogs that are overweight have a higher risk of heart problems than their trimmer friends. And they're more likely to have skin and respiratory conditions, as well as serious illnesses like arthritis and diabetes.

It's common for dogs to gain a little weight as they get older because their metabolisms gradually slow down. But it's worth keeping them lean. Whether your dog is five or 14, he should weigh about the same as he did on his first birthday, says William Fortney, D.V.M., staff veterinarian at Kansas State University's Veterinary Teaching Hospital in Manhattan.

Neutering doesn't cause dogs to get porky. Age doesn't have a big impact. Neither does the food you buy. The main reason dogs get fat is that they have overindulgent owners who put a little too much in the food bowl and hand over too many treats.

IS YOUR DOG A HEALTHY WEIGHT?

Check your dog's weight by feeling his ribs. If you can't see or feel his ribs he's overweight. By contrast, if the ribs are too prominent, he's underweight.

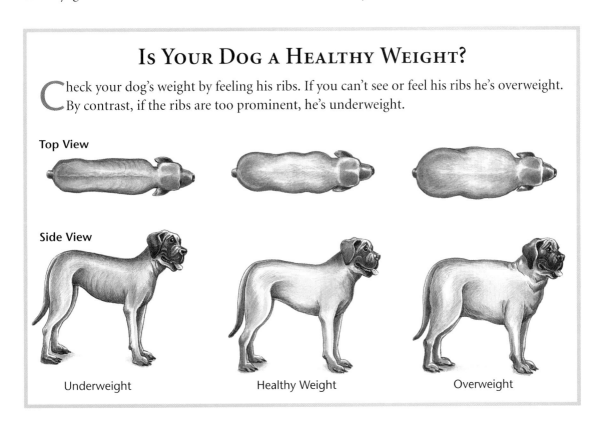

Top View

Side View

Underweight   Healthy Weight   Overweight

If you're wondering whether your dog has made the transition from stocky to rotund, take a look at his belly. "It should curve upward from the rib cage toward the tail rather than hanging down," says Karen Mateyak, D.V.M., a veterinarian in private practice in Brooklyn, New York. Then look at your dog from behind—you should be able to discern a "waist" where the sides go in just behind the ribs. "If your dog looks like a cylinder from behind, he's too fat," says Dr. Mateyak.

Take your dog to the vet before beginning a weight loss program to check that there isn't any underlying disease causing the weight gain.

The formula for losing weight is as simple for dogs as it is for people: They have to take in fewer calories and burn more with exercise. Your dog isn't going to get there by himself, however. He needs you, his personal trainer, to set the pace. Here's how to do it right.

Feed him less, but more often. Start by reducing the amount of food that you give your dog by about 20 percent. He's not trying to fit into a suit for a job interview, so there's no need for crash diets. Of course, your dog probably takes his food very seriously, and even a slight reduction may make him feel like he's starving all the time. One way to keep him satisfied is to feed him more often, but give smaller amounts, says Dr. Mateyak. Your dog will probably never notice that he's getting less overall, she explains.

Pudgy Pooch Spa

Portly guests of the Cozy Inn Pet Resort and Spa in Stahlstown, Pennsylvania, can participate in a weight-loss program designed by one of the resort's resident veterinarians. "A lot of clients will go on a weight-loss program of their own, and drop off their pets at the resort to lose weight too," says Carol Boerio-Croft, owner of the spa.

Each guest enrolled in the program gets a thorough physical exam and a customized weight-loss plan, which involves exercise, massage therapy, whirlpool baths, and a specialized diet. This program is put together by a vet and is based on the results of the physical exam, blood tests, and an interview with each dog's owner.

The resort's facilities include an in-ground bone-shaped pool, a warm whirlpool bath, a 24 acre off-leash park, and a half-mile aerobics/nature walk designed to help get the pets' hearts pumping.

Once dogs are fit and trim and ready to return home, owners are encouraged to modify their dogs' diet (especially by reducing treats) to keep their dogs' weight down to what it should be.

Billie, a Labrador-mix, dropped 50 pounds at the Cozy Inn. When he came to the spa he was about 130 pounds and had little energy and no desire to play.

Billie reduced down to a sleek 80 pounds. "He's now a big, beautiful dog with a high energy level and loves to play," says Boerio-Croft.

Slow his eating. When your dog hangs around you with a mournful look on his face after he's cleaned out his bowl, don't be fooled into thinking he needs more food. Food-loving canines often eat at breakneck speed and then look around for more. Get your dog to take time over his food by dividing each of his meals into two or three smaller ones. Place each portion of

BREED SPECIFIC

Basset hounds, Labrador retrievers, bulldogs, and Shetland sheepdogs all have a tendency to put on weight.

food in a different part of the room. This will make him think he's eaten more and he won't instantly want some treats.

Give him a special food. There are a number of dog foods designed specifically for weight loss. They're lower in fat and higher in fiber than regular foods. Fiber is very filling and provides almost no calories, Dr. Fortney explains. Fat, on the other hand, is extremely high in calories, and buying a low-fat food is one of the easiest ways to help your dog lose weight.

Dogs don't always take well to changes in their diets and will sometimes get diarrhea when you switch foods, Dr. Fortney adds. One way to prevent this is to make the change gradually, mixing in some of the new food with some of the old. Doing this slowly over a period of weeks, increasing the new food every day, will help ensure that his tummy stays calm.

Give him some vegetables. Dogs are natural meat-eaters, but they don't mind eating vegetables now and then. In fact, you can easily reduce the calories your dog consumes by substituting some chopped, raw vegetables for some of his regular food, says Dr. Fortney.

Trim the treats. The last thing your dog needs when you're trying to help him lose weight is extra treats to nosh on. But if you can't resist—and most of us can't—at least give him

low-calorie biscuits, preferably broken into small pieces. A single biscuit could easily last all day, says Dr. Mateyak. Your dog won't be upset at the smaller amount, she adds. "The fact that you've given him something is what really makes him happy." You don't even have to give him "extra" treats, says Dr. Fortney. Set aside some of his usual kibble, then dole it out during the day as a snack.

Get out and about. Taking a walk a couple of times a day is one of the best ways to keep your dog's weight down. Of course, if he hasn't been moving much lately, you don't want to go all-out all at once. Take some short, slow walks to give his muscles and lungs a chance to adjust. Then pick up the pace. The faster you walk and the more distance you cover, the more the pounds will fall away. Most dogs need about 15 to 30 minutes of exercise twice a day.

This airborne fox terrier-mix gets a lot of vigorous exercise and is unlikely to ever be overweight.

133

Solving Behavior Problems

No one has perfect manners, and our dogs are no exception. They bark at midnight, chew on furniture, or make messes where they shouldn't. Dogs don't mean any harm when they misbehave. Usually there's something wrong, and their bad behavior is a valuable way of letting you know they're not happy. Once you know what's causing your dog to act up, finding a solution won't be difficult—and you'll soon be enjoying a more confident and contented companion.

Aggression

For dogs, aggression is just another form of communication, like barking or wagging their tails. The message it sends, of course, is much more serious. Similar to human anger, aggression is a dog's way of setting boundaries. In the wild, dogs depended on aggression to protect their possessions—such as food—from other dogs, and also to protect the pack from intruders and themselves from bodily harm.

What's acceptable in the wild, however, isn't appropriate in the living room. Whether your dog occasionally gives a low rumble when you walk past his food, or actually snarls or snaps at people, what he's doing is trying to assume a position of control, and that can be worrisome, says Mary R. Burch, Ph.D., a certified applied animal behaviorist in Tallahassee, Florida. Aggression is potentially the most serious behavior problem dog owners will ever have to deal with, and it needs to be stopped quickly before it escalates.

There are many different forms of aggression, and how you approach your dog's problem will depend on which type of aggression he shows. For example, dogs that bark at or ac-

This foxhound displays protective aggression by barking at intruders.

tually threaten visitors are showing "protective aggression." Dogs that threaten their owners are showing "dominance aggression"—they're trying to take over as leader of the family. And dogs that only get aggressive when they're frightened are showing "fear-related aggression." Other dogs only become aggressive as a result of "pain-related aggression." Some dogs exhibit "predatory aggression" when they see a fast-moving object that they feel compelled to chase.

Ultimately, it doesn't matter what's making your dog aggressive because any type of aggression toward humans or other pets is serious. And it never goes away on its own. If anything, aggressive behavior tends to get worse over time if it's not addressed, says Linda Goodloe, Ph.D., an animal behaviorist in New York City.

It's a good idea to work with a trainer when your dog first starts acting aggressively. But in some cases, there are things you can do to keep your dog calmer, and, more importantly, help him understand his place in the family. Here's what experts advise.

Give yourself a promotion. Aggression sometimes occurs when dogs think their owners are weak and in need of leadership, says Dr. Burch. If you give your dog too much attention or cater to his every desire, he may get the idea that he's the master instead of you. And he'll use aggression to keep you in line.

Whether you have a strong-willed German shepherd or an assertive toy poodle, it's essential to establish yourself as the "top dog" in the family. This means taking care of your wants and desires before thinking about what your dog wants. Make him sit before you let him outside. Only give him treats after he has obeyed your command to lie down. The idea is to make him understand that he has to work for you, not the other way around.

Get him off the furniture. It's a lot of fun to watch TV or read with your dog next to you on the couch. And dogs love soft places to sleep. But there's a problem with letting dogs on the furniture. In the wild, high sleeping grounds were always taken by the pack leader. Letting your dog on the furniture will get him thinking that he's your equal—or your boss. Getting him off the furniture and onto the floor will re-inforce your dog's subordinate position in the family pack.

Show him the world. Some aggression problems are caused by fear of the unknown, which is why veterinarians recommend intro-ducing dogs to a wide variety of people, places, and things, preferably from the time they're young. The more your dog encounters—busy streets, strange people, delivery trucks, cars going by—the less likely he is to be fearful and aggressive later on.

Even older dogs that are already showing signs of fear can be taught to be more accepting of new people and situations. Obedience classes will help build their confidence and get them used to other people and other dogs. And it doesn't hurt to act happy and confident your-self. Dogs take many of their cues from us. When you're relaxed, your dog will be too.

Make the scary safe. It's not uncommon for dogs to be fearful—and aggressive—only at certain times, such as when they're in the vet-

Regular obedience drills reduce this Dalmatian-mix's aggression by reinforcing his owner's role as leader.

erinarian's office. You can often overcome this type of aggression by helping them form more positive associations with whatever it is they're afraid of.

Suppose your dog hates going to the veteri-narian, but loves going for rides in a car. Once a week or so, take him for a ride to the vet's. Don't take him in, however. Just park in front of the office and maybe give your dog a treat. Then drive back home. A few days later, make the trip again. This time bring him in with you—not for a checkup, but just so he can check things out while you chat with the receptionists. Give him a treat and then leave again. If you keep doing this, he'll gradually realize that going to the vet's means treats and a drive. He'll associate the place with pleasure instead of fear. Then, when he really does need a checkup, he'll be less likely to misbehave.

Cut the coddling. When your dog is acting fearful and aggressive, the last thing you want to do is make a fuss over him. This will only aggravate the problem because it rewards him for bad behavior. If your dog starts acting aggressively toward people or other dogs, he should be given a verbal or a leash correction, and should not be rewarded for his bad behavior by being coddled or reassured.

Teach him to welcome visitors. Many dogs are protective of their families and their homes, and some go nearly ballistic when people come to the door. What you want to do is teach them that visitors are welcome and aren't a threat. The easiest way to do this is to act excited and happy when people come to the door, says Dr. Burch. This will naturally cause your dog to let his guard down a little and be more accepting of the "intruder."

BREED SPECIFIC

The type of aggression a dog displays is partly influenced by what he was originally bred to do. Hunting breeds such as hounds and this Norwich terrier are prone to predatory aggression, in which they chase other animals. Some terriers that were originally bred as dog-fighters may exhibit dog-to-dog aggression. And dogs such as Rottweilers and Doberman pinschers may show signs of protective aggression because they were bred to guard livestock and property.

You can also train dogs to be less aggressive toward visitors, says Dr. Burch. The next time a visitor comes in ask her to happily greet you. If your dog is agreeable, have her play with him for a while, offer him a treat, and pet him. (Remember never to force yourself or anyone else on a dog who's behaving with obvious aggression.) Over time, your dog will discover that visitors can be fun.

Of course, dogs that are extremely aggressive aren't going to warm up to anyone in just a few visits, and forcing them to be social isn't going to work. Dogs that are aggressive toward visitors must be treated by an expert.

Discourage aggressive play. Starting when your dog is a puppy, it's best to avoid aggressive games and only play those that will reinforce the notion that your dog should be doing things for you, such as fetching, in which he'll be trained to bring you a ball or stick and drop it on command. Fetch is the safest game people can play with their dogs, while at the same time letting them get some really good exercise, says Kathy Diamond Davis, a trainer in Oklahoma City.

Relieve his pain. If a normally placid dog suddenly acts aggressively, chances are he's in pain. "Dogs who are in pain often respond with aggression to handling or being approached," says Dr. Burch. A trip to the vet will relieve his pain, and your dog should soon be back to his old cheerful self.

FAST FIX In male dogs especially, aggressive behavior is often amplified by high levels of sex hormones. Having dogs spayed or neutered can reduce or even eliminate aggression altogether.

Barking

Dogs bark for many reasons. They bark to show excitement or happiness, to let you know they're hungry, or to say they want to play. They bark to warn off "intruders," like the mailman or guests at the door. Sometimes they bark for no other reason than they're bored, and sounding off keeps them entertained.

"Barking is the way early dogs communicated with others in the pack," says Mary R. Burch, Ph.D., a certified applied animal behaviorist in Tallahassee, Florida. "They barked to give warnings or provide information about their location."

Barking is a dog's natural means of communication, and it can be both lovable and infuriating. While some dogs rarely bark, others do it all the time, and no one appreciates the racket, least of all the neighbors who have to listen to it when you're at work all day. It isn't possible to stop dogs from barking entirely, but there are ways to keep them a little bit quieter. Here's what experts recommend.

Distract them from their noisemaking. Dogs love to bark, but they love your approval more. Letting your dog know you're not pleased with his noisemak-

Rattling a tin can half-filled with metal makes a sound dogs dislike and will help stop them barking.

The Hero Hudson

Barking can be a really good trait in a dog, as a cat named Zoe can attest. Zoe managed to crawl inside the clothes dryer one day. Without realizing that Zoe was inside, her owner, Liz Beaumont turned on the dryer. That's when Hudson, Beaumont's dog, started barking.

"At first I thought Hudson wanted to go outside, but he just kept barking and staring at the machine," Beaumont told Reuters News Service. Finally, she realized something was wrong, and opened the clothes dryer. There was Zoe, a little scorched, but, ultimately, none the worse for wear.

PUPPY DOG TALES

ing can be a powerful incentive to make him stop. However, yelling at him isn't the best approach because he'll just think you're joining in the fun. A better approach is to toss a length of chain—or an aluminum or tin can half-filled with metal or pennies—in your dog's general direction. The clattering sound will startle him into silence. Once he stops barking, praise him. Over time your dog will learn that silence brings more rewards than noise.

Drown out the excitement. Dogs often bark because there's something going on outside that's getting their attention. For example, it could be the barking dog next door, who's encouraging your dog to bark back an answer. One way to keep dogs a little quieter is to block or at least mask the sounds—by leaving on a radio when you leave the house, or closing

WHAT DOES THAT BARK MEAN?

Experts still aren't sure why dogs bark and what they're trying to say. But anyone who's been around dogs knows they have many different barks. Some are shrill while others are deep. Dogs may bark rapidly in succession, or do it slowly and steadily.

There are three different kinds of barks, says Linda Goodloe, Ph.D., a certified applied animal behaviorist in New York City.

• Fast and furious—nuisance barking. This is how dogs sometimes react to people or dogs that are moving past or coming toward them.

• Strong and steady—watchdog barking. This is how dogs may respond to intruders who are approaching their turf. They'll also give strong, steady barks when they hear noises outside.

• Urgent and anxious—separation barking. Dogs sometimes bark when they're alone and feeling lonely. This kind of barking has a nervous, anxious quality.

windows in the rooms where they spend their days. The less they hear, the less likely they'll be to bark.

Change the scenery. What dogs see also stimulates barking. Anything from a squirrel scuttling across the yard to the sight of the neighbor's cat can trigger a barking outburst. Closing the blinds will eliminate at least one source of excitement and should keep things a little quieter. If that doesn't work, try keeping your dog in a secluded part of the house with some toys to occupy him when you're not home, says Dr. Burch.

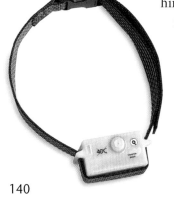

A citronella collar is an effective way to quickly distract your dog from barking.

FAST FIX Persistent barkers can sometimes be made to stop with a citronella collar. These bark-activated collars release a brief burst of citronella, a natural plant extract. It's harmless, but dogs don't like the smell, and the *psst* sound gets their attention, causing them to quieten down and listen. After a while, your dog will get the idea that barking has slightly odoriferous consequences. Citronella collars are effective about 70 percent of the time for problem barkers when they are used correctly, says Linda Goodloe, Ph.D., a certified applied animal behaviorist in New York City.

Bring him inside. Even if you have a comfortable, fenced yard, it's not a good idea to leave your dog outside when you're not going to be around. The combination of sights and sounds and the boredom of being left alone can trigger hours of non-stop, monotonous barking. It's a good idea to keep dogs inside when you're gone,

says Dr. Burch. Or at least bring them inside during high-bark times—when the kids get out of school, for example, or when the mailman is making his rounds.

Wear him out. Dogs that have a lot of energy and not a lot of outlets for it will often bark simply because they're bored and in need of excitement. Giving your dog a lot of exercise will help wear him out—and tired dogs are unlikely to be barking dogs. Also, play games with your dog, such as throwing a ball or Frisbee, as often as possible. This will prevent him barking out of excess energy or boredom.

Hire some help. Unless you spend your days at home, your dog is going to be alone a lot of the time. Dogs crave company, and being alone can be stressful and lonely—feelings they try to alleviate by barking. If you aren't able to keep your dog company during the day, you may want to hire a professional pet sitter—or even someone from the neighborhood—to come by once or twice a day and let him out. The extra exercise will help tire him out, and the extra company will break up the boredom and curb his urge to bark.

BREED SPECIFIC

Breeds such as Lhasa Apsos, Rottweilers, German shepherds and American Eskimo dogs have been molded for centuries to alert their masters to the approach of strangers. Herding dogs like Shetland sheepdogs and Border collies, and hunting dogs like beagles and dachshunds also have a lot to say.

Give him something else to do. Dogs sometimes get bored with their own company, just like people do. One way to keep them entertained is to give them toys they can play with when they're alone. Experts often recommend giving problem barkers hollow rubber toys, which you can fill with cream cheese or peanut butter. Dogs will often spend hours trying to get to the goodies inside. They'll have a great time and, of course, will be much too preoccupied to bark.

Send him to school. Barking dogs are often very bored dogs, says Dr. Burch, who recommends obedience training for all problem barkers. Obedience training gives your dog a feeling that he has a job to do in life (obey his owner), and this helps to settle his anxiety and relieve his boredom. "Obedience training provides your dog with a sense of purpose as well as a new set of skills for everyday living," says Dr. Burch.

Playing with your dog will help prevent boredom barking.

Destructiveness

Many dogs, from the most refined poodle to the heartiest mutt, seem to have a secret side. When you're home your dog is always on his best behavior. But when you leave for work or go to bed, his personality changes and he shows his dark side—as you later discover when you find your tattered shirt, chewed shoes, and dug-up plants.

It's normal for puppies to chew, so your first task, after buying a food bowl, a tiny collar, and a chew toy, is to get your possessions off the floor and out of jaw-range. But destructive behavior has no age limits. Some older dogs, after years of good behavior, suddenly seem to forget their lessons and go on a rampage. They're not being spiteful or trying to punish you for leaving them at home all day. They're just finding the most convenient outlet for their emotions.

Don't Leave Me

Dogs don't show their emotions the way people do, so we sometimes forget that they experience many of the same feelings, such as anxiety, frustration, and boredom. They can't tell you when they're upset, but they can show you—sometimes with destructive behavior.

It's not a coincidence that dogs are usually at their most destructive when they're left alone, says Daniela Ortner, an animal behaviorist in Los Angeles, California. Until humans came on the scene, dogs always lived in packs, and they don't like spending time alone. In your dog's eyes, you're part of his pack, and when you leave the house, he may feel abandoned. As his anxiety mounts he may experience the canine equivalent of temporary insanity and begin annihilating everything within reach. It's his way of working out bad feelings. For more information on separation anxiety see pages 158 to 159.

Unless you spend your days at home, there's no easy way to monitor your dog's goings-on. It takes time and patience, but there are ways to help him cope with being on his own.

Enroll your dog in doggie day care. The extra attention will make him less anxious—and less destructive.

CHEW TOYS

Dogs can often be diverted by chew toys. There is a wide variety available from pet supply stores and catalogs.

Rope/nylon tug toy

Chocolate dog pull

Dumbbell

Play ball and rope

Hedgehog squeeze toy

Plush toy

Cheese ball

Kong toy

Find him a job. Dogs who are confident and secure are much less likely to become destructive when they're alone. A great way to boost your dog's ego is to give him something to do—anything from canine sports like flyball to visiting hospitals or nursing homes. Also, active dogs are tired dogs, so they're more likely to sleep than look for trouble when you're gone, says Patricia McConnell, Ph.D., a certified animal behaviorist in Black Earth, Wisconsin.

Dogs need special training for therapy-dog work. That's not a bad thing, because many dogs enjoy obedience training, and especially the praise that comes from doing a good job.

Keep his jaws busy. One reason dogs chew when they're upset is because that's their way of relieving tension, and also of passing the time. One of the best ways to stop a destructive dog who enjoys chewing is to give him acceptable alternatives, like chew toys or tennis balls, says Steven Appelbaum, an animal behaviorist in Northridge, California. A good choice is the Kong toy, says Dr. McConnell. Made of stout rubber with a hollow cavity inside, these are designed to hold small amounts of food, like cheese or a spoonful of peanut butter. Dogs can happily spend hours just trying to get the food out of the hole.

When choosing chew toys, avoid discarded socks or shoes. Your dog can't tell the difference between old, rejected slippers and brand-new pumps. If you let him think one shoe is acceptable, he'll conclude that all shoes are fair game.

Use a deterrent. Some dogs have a favorite object—anything from a piano leg to the corner of a door frame—and will keep returning to chew the life out of it. Spraying the object with something that tastes or smells bad, such as Bitter Apple or citronella, available in pet supply stores, will help keep them away.

Another approach is to booby-trap the things your dog chews—for example, by putting coins in an empty soda can and tying it to the object of his desire. When he grabs it, the noise will startle him and he may think twice about chewing it next time.

Give him his own space. Dogs naturally gravitate to small, enclosed, den-like spaces, especially when they're anxious. In fact, many dogs feel insecure when they have the run of the house—they don't know what to do with all that space. Try confining your dog in a small room or gradually get him used to being crated when you're not home. This can make him feel much safer and more secure, so he's less likely to run amok.

Sabotage his digging. Some dogs get destructive in the house; others love tearing up the yard. It's extremely hard to discourage a dog that digs digging, but you can make it harder for him by burying lava rock in the area, since he won't like the way it feels when he hits it, says Appelbaum. Or try cutting his nails so that digging feels uncomfortable—but don't cut them so short that you damage the sensitive quick.

Drop by occasionally. If you're lucky enough to live close to work, you can always drop by at lunchtime. When you visit your dog during the day, his isolation is interrupted, and

This bearded collie is burning tremendous amounts of energy. The more he plays and exercises the less likely he is to be distressed and destructive.

he'll be less likely to be anxious when you're gone. When you're not able to get away from work, you might want to arrange with a neighbor or a professional dog sitter to drop by your home during the day. Giving your dog someone to play with, even if it's only for a few minutes, will help keep him entertained while taking his mind off your belongings, says Ortner.

Wear him out. While dogs often use destructive behavior as a way of defusing stress, they also do it simply because they have more energy than they know what to do with. A good solution is to give him a lot of exercise just before you leave in the morning and again when you get home at night, says Dr. McConnell. A dog who's used up all his energy is much less likely to be destructive.

BREED SPECIFIC

Some dogs have been bred to work for hours a day without rest, such as Border collies, Siberian huskies (left), flat-coat retrievers and Airedales. They have energy they need to burn, and tend to be destructive when they're kept inside with nothing to do.

Fear

Even a normally happy and confident dog will be panicked and frightened at times. Loud noises, strange people, or unfamiliar objects alarm many dogs. Others are frightened by specific things—a flight of stairs, for example, or the rustle of newspaper. Sometimes it seems there's just no rhyme or reason to why a dog gets spooked. He may cower under the table when there's a thunderstorm, but bound around happily at the sound of firecrackers, says Barbara S. Simpson, D.V.M., Ph.D., a certified applied animal behaviorist in Southern Pines, North Carolina.

It's easy to figure out when dogs are fearful, but it's never easy to teach them to cope. This can be a slow process, so you'll need to be patient and persistent. Whether your dog is generally fearful, or just afraid of a specific thing, here's what the experts recommend.

Get him used to it. A dog that is used to the hustle and bustle of daily life, the noise of traffic, the sound of doors slamming, or strangers stroking him in the street will be more able to take life in stride than a dog who's coddled and protected from the world around him. Socialize your dog early in his life, gradually introducing him to people, sounds, and situations that he's sure to encounter later on. And be sure to praise him when he handles a new encounter or experience well.

Act naturally. Dogs often take their cue from their owners and the people around them. If your body language says you're scared in a particular situation, it's likely your dog will pick up on this and be apprehensive, too. Act calm and unconcerned, and your dog will be less likely to be fearful.

Save the hugs for later. Throwing your arms around a frightened dog and speaking soothingly may be the instinctive thing to do, but try to hold back, experts advise. He'll misunderstand this and think you're praising him for acting scared.

Your best bet is to distract him from whatever is causing his anxiety. Giving him a food treat or playing with him will help. And if something scary does happen and he copes well, that's the time to praise and hug.

Build his confidence. Dogs that are nervous and easily frightened often improve when given obedience training. Obedience training

CALL FOR HELP

When your attempts at alleviating your dog's fear don't get results, ask a dog trainer for help, says Barbara Simpson, a certified animal behaviorist in Southern Pines, North Carolina. Dogs who can't be calmed can be a danger to themselves and to those around them. A trainer may recommend a course of behavioral modification, in which your dog is gradually exposed to what scares him until it ceases to do so. In some case, it may be necessary for your dog to be given anti-anxiety drugs by your veterinarian, as well.

Playing a game along with reconditioning will help take a dog's mind off something that's frightened him. This miniature fox terrier is being distracted by a game so that he is less fearful of what was bothering him.

builds confidence, which in turn gives your dog the fortitude to cope calmly with many different situations.

Training not only socializes him to other people and dogs, it helps him recognize that you're in charge, and able to make many decisions for him. "If he thinks he's the little king of the household and it's his job to make all the decisions, he'll often show fear," says Patrick Melese, D.V.M., a certified applied animal behaviorist in San Diego, California.

Once your dog knows he doesn't have to carry the world on his shoulders, he'll grow in confidence. None of this will happen overnight, so be prepared to invest some time and patience in regular training sessions over a period of weeks or months.

Condition him to the big bang. Loud sounds can send some dogs into a complete frenzy. It could be because dogs' hearing is much more acute than humans', and the rumble of thunder must seem like the house is falling in.

A great way to help your dog get over his fear of loud noises is with a technique called reconditioning, says Dr. Melese. This method will help your dog learn to associate something pleasant with the sound.

Start by recording the sound your dog is afraid of. Play it near him in two to five minute sessions, a couple of times a day, "Start with a low volume, one that doesn't bother him much," says Dr. Melese. "Play it in different rooms of the house so he thinks, 'Hey, I can hear this sound anywhere!' Then slowly increase the volume." If he acts unhappy, backtrack and lower the volume. When he relaxes again, slowly increase the level.

While your dog is listening to the scary sound, do something fun, like toss a ball or throw a stick. Eventually, he'll learn to think

Because he's used to new situations, meeting different people and animals, this Tibetan terrier takes greeting these puppies in his stride.

Grand Canyon Dog

At the tender age of eight weeks, a Border collie-mix, later named L. B. Franks, was found by Margaret Hench at the bottom of the Grand Canyon. He was covered with mange, starving, had a fractured leg and a broken tail, and two mysterious scratches on the back of his neck.

The area where L. B. was found has sheer walls, with the river a full mile below the canyon's rim. No one know how he survived on the canyon's floor, but a vet estimated that he'd gone at least three days without food.

The mystery of how L. B. got there was solved by the scratches on the back of his neck: They were talon marks. A golden eagle, a common bird in the area, had scooped L. B. up at the rim and dropped him down below.

Despite his amazing adventure, L. B. Franks grew up to be a calm, well-adjusted dog. He does therapy work with children and lives happily with Margaret Hench and her husband Bob, who adopted him.

about playtime when he hears the noise and won't be as terrified. You can't expect him to learn to love the sound, but you can teach him not to over-react to it.

Broaden his experiences. Dogs are naturally companionable creatures, but they need to work at getting used to people with loud voices, kids with inquisitive fingers, or workmen with strange tools.

When a dog is intimidated by people he's never met, he probably didn't get a lot of attention from humans when he was a pup. The best thing is a preventive approach, started early in life if possible.

Whether you have a puppy or an older dog, expose him gradually to different people so he learns not to fear strangers. And expose him to people in different situations too, like a busy shopping mall. The broader his experiences with people, the less frightening his world will be.

Try some play acting. People who look unusual to a dog can also trigger a fear response. People holding umbrellas, wearing bulky clothing, or even walking with a cane or crutch can cause fear in some dogs.

The best way to deal with your dog's fear of people who look unusual is to do a bit of play acting at home, where the "weird person" approaches your dog slowly. Enlist the aid of a friend or two and create the "characters" you've seen him get so upset about.

Pay the vet a social call. If it's the veterinarian that your dog dreads and no one else, it's because he's come to associate the vet with something unpleasant, says Dr. Melese. Your vet is important to your dog's well-being, so when visits to the vet have turned into a nightmare, you will need to take steps to improve things.

Set up an appointment with your veterinarian, preferably at a quiet time of day. Ask your vet to give your dog a few treats and make friends with him, and to handle him in a "non-vet" way.

Get him used to touch. Some dogs are fearful of being touched and will pull away or cower when someone reaches out to them. "Some dogs are head-shy," says Dr. Melese. "When someone moves their hand near the head of one of these dogs, the dog gets scared."

From the time he was young this Border collie was handled by a lot of different people. He learned to enjoy and not fear the attention.

Your dog is not going to be able to get through life without being touched, so you'll want to help him get over this problem. You can help him to associate hands with good things by getting strangers to give him treats and scratches behind the ear.

Show him it's normal. Everyday objects give some dogs the creeps. A pile of washing in the laundry or a chair on the porch can inexplicably push a dog's alarm button.

A dog becomes afraid of an inanimate object for two reasons. He might have never seen the object before and think it's plain weird-looking. Or the object did some-

thing that scared the dickens out of him. Either way, your dog hates the thing and won't go near it. He'll act afraid every time he sees it.

Once your dog realizes that the "strange" object is here to stay, he'll usually get over his fear of it, says Dr. Melese. Seeing you touching and using the object will help to reassure him that it's not out to get you and it's not out to get him.

If your dog really hates a machine, such as a vacuum cleaner, experts recommend you don't force him to love it. What you can do is give him an escape route or put him in an area of the house where he can only hear it from a distance.

In time, your dog will learn that just as you emerge unscathed from being around this "monster," so will he.

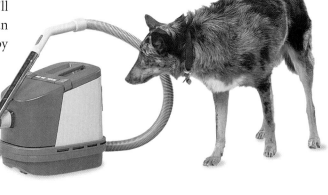

This collie-cattle dog-cross is very wary of the vacuum cleaner. When it's being used, his owner puts him in an area of the house where he can only hear it from a distance.

148

Fussy Eating

Dogs have a reputation for eating anything that drops in their bowls—or on the kitchen floor—but this isn't always the case. Some dogs are naturally picky and will sniff their food and then walk away if it isn't to their liking. Others have developed a taste for human food, and dry kibble has lost its appeal. And some dogs simply don't like what you're giving them and are fed up to the back teeth with getting the same chow day after day.

Giving food the cold shoulder can also be a result of an owner not knowing how much their dog really needs to eat. Every dog has a different capacity for food. Learning what's normal for your dog will stop you from foisting food on her when she's simply not hungry, explains Peter Borchelt, Ph.D., a certified applied animal behaviorist at Animal Behavior Associates in Brooklyn, New York. A dog that weighs five pounds will need about 250 calories a day, while a 100 pound dog will need about 2,400 calories.

Whatever the reason for your dog's indifference, there are ways to help suppertime become the pleasurable event it should be. Here's what experts advise.

Find the right flavor. Sometimes the easiest way to overcome fussy eating is to find a food your dog likes, says Dr. Borchelt. Some people give their dogs one particular brand with never a thought as to whether or not their pets actually like it. "If you had an infant who hated chicken and spinach, you wouldn't try to force them on him," says Dr. Borchelt. "You'd try turkey and carrots instead."

CALL FOR HELP

It's not unusual for dogs to go a day without eating, especially when you're encouraging them to try some new foods. But when a food-loving pet suddenly stops eating for two days or more, you should call your vet. Lost appetite is a common symptom of many serious illnesses, and you'll want to get a checkup right away.

If your dog has never been overly enthusiastic about eating, try some different foods, Dr. Borchelt suggests. Keep trying new brands or combinations until you find a food she likes. When you do, stick with it, he advises. Many dogs appreciate getting the same meal every day. There's no reason to change foods as long as she seems happy with what she's getting.

Wean her off human food. Dogs that are used to people food often turn up their noses at dog food, says Daniela Ortner, an animal behaviorist in Los Angeles. This isn't only because lamb chops taste a lot better than dry kibble. "It becomes a social thing," says Dr. Borchelt. In other words, your dog may enjoy eating human foods simply because you are there when she eats them.

Even if you don't mind having your dog at the dinner table, it's not a good idea to hand over scraps, says Dr. Borchelt. Human foods won't provide all the nutrients your dog needs.

In addition, they may be a little too rich for a dog's digestive tract to handle.

It's not always easy to persuade dogs to give up their taste for human food and start eating dog food again. To make the switch, gradually increase the proportion of dog food to human food in her diet. At first, you may want to feed her about 80 percent of what she's used to combined with 20 percent of the food you want her to eat. After a day or two, increase the percentage of dog food in the mix. Keep doing this until she's eating mainly dog food. To prevent your dog from picking out her favorites and eschewing the rest, it's a good idea to put the different foods, along with a little warm water, in a blender and really stir them up.

Stay nearby when she eats. Since your dog's taste for human food is motivated partly by her desire to be close to you, you can encourage her appetite simply by being nearby. After a few days (or in some

Like this Old English sheepdog-Border collie-cross, some dogs crave company at meals and won't eat alone.

cases, weeks) gradually put yourself more and more out of the picture. Eventually she'll learn to eat her food without your company.

Limit the length of mealtimes. Some dogs feel free to walk away from their food because they know it—or something even better—is going to be there the next time they approach their bowl. Feeding your dog at the same time every day will help "train" her appetite so she's hungry and ready when you want her to be. Take your dog's food away if she doesn't eat it in 30 minutes. This will help her learn that if she doesn't eat quickly, she'll miss the opportunity.

Make her meals interesting. Some dogs are content to eat the same dry kibble for breakfast and dinner. Others start getting fussy because they crave some variety, says Dr. Borchelt. He recommends making your dog's meals more exciting—by mixing wet and dry food together, for example, or giving one type of food in the morning and another type in the evening.

There's nothing wrong with giving dogs treats now and then, especially when they've temporarily lost their appetites because they're feeling ill, says Robin Kovary, a dog trainer, behavioral consultant, and director of the American Dog Trainer's Network in New York City. One way to encourage your dog to eat is to sprinkle parmesan cheese on her dinner. Or give her a little bit of powdered freeze-dried liver or chicken broth. Just don't pamper her too much, Kovary adds. "There is a risk that your dog will learn to hold out for the yummy stuff."

Shop for strong smells. Smell has a lot to do with food appeal, too, so go for a food that has a powerful aroma. Canned foods have the

WHAT FOOD IS BEST?

The basic types of commercial dog food are dry, semi-moist, and canned. There are also three quality levels—generic, popular, and premium. Dry foods have the highest energy content, followed by semi-moist and canned moist. Canned moist foods and semi-moist foods have a strong aroma and flavor that dogs particularly like. What's important is to get the balance of nutrients right for your dog, taking into account her breed, age, size, and levels of activity—and this may mean feeding her a mixture of types. Quality level is another important consideration. Generic

| Dry | Semi-moist | Moist canned |

foods are low in price, but offer the lowest nutritional value, while popular brands are made to variable formulations that may change from batch to batch. Premium foods are designed to provide optimal nutrition. Whatever you choose, check the label to see that it meets standards set by the American Association of Feed Control Officials.

strongest smell, followed by semi-moist, with dry foods being the least odoriferous. Canned foods contain a variety of meat, fish, and cereal-based products, some smellier than others. You'll need to test out a few to see which ones have your dog drooling in anticipation. While a liver-based product may have her munching contentedly, a chicken-based one may leave her decidedly unimpressed.

Dangerous Treats

Even dogs that routinely walk away from a full food bowl will stand up and take notice when they're offered a delectable treat—which is why people sometimes try to tempt them with the most toothsome treat of all—a little bit of

chocolate. Dogs love chocolate, but it's about the worst food they can have, says Janice M. Posnikoff, D.V.M., a veterinarian in private practice in Tustin, California. Chocolate contains a compound called theobromine, which can cause severe, life-threatening diarrhea. Baking chocolate is especially bad for dogs because it contains nearly nine times more theobromine than milk chocolate.

The problem with chocolate, apart from its tempting taste, is its smell: Dogs can smell chocolate all the way across a room, and will go to surprising lengths—like tearing open packages or raiding the counter—to get a taste. To keep your dog safe, be sure to keep chocolate well out of reach—and preferably behind closed doors, says Dr. Posnikoff.

Housesoiling

Puddle-jumping is a common hazard when you're housebreaking a puppy, but when a normally well-behaved adult dog starts housesoiling, you'll need to work out why.

Indoor indiscretions often occur when dogs try to wait, but can't. Some physical problems can make it hard for dogs to control themselves. More often, accidents occur when dogs are left inside for too long. "Even an adult dog can't go all day and into the evening without relieving herself," says Jeannene Kutsukos, a dog trainer at Pro Dog Training in Springfield, Illinois.

Even well-intentioned dogs will sometimes opt for doing their business inside, adds Daniel Q. Estep, Ph.D., a certified applied animal behaviorist in Littleton, Colorado. For example, a dog may have trouble making a pit stop in deep snow. "She may decide, 'Hey, going in the house is much more convenient for me than going outside where it is unpleasant. I think I'll go in the house from now on,'" he says.

Whatever the reason for your dog's sudden change in behavior, housesoiling is seldom a very complicated problem and can usually be stopped quickly.

A regular schedule for walks and meals will help prevent accidents.

Move her food bowl. Dogs are naturally reluctant to soil the area where they eat or drink. Putting her food bowl near a favorite urination spot will often make her wait until she can use the "approved" location.

Get her used to a crate. Dogs dislike messing where they sleep, says Kutsukos. Crating your dog when you're gone will encourage her to wait until you can let her out to do her business. If your dog has never been crated, talk to a trainer or your vet before confining her. Most dogs don't mind crates, but they can get scared when put in one for the first time. Once they're used to it, most dogs enjoy the comfort that crates provide.

Get rid of the smell. Dogs are drawn to the smell of urine, and will often return to the scene of the crime unless you remove every trace of the scent. Household cleaners often make things worse because the smell of ammonia resembles that of urine, says Kutsukos. Treat the area with an odor-neutralizer, available from pet supply stores. Or try spraying citronella—a natural plant extract that has a smell dogs dislike— twice a week on the areas your dog has messed.

Stick to a schedule. Dogs respond best to a regular schedule. Try to feed your dog at the same times each day and, when possible, let her out at the same times each day. When she knows that "her" time is approaching, she'll be more likely to follow the proper procedure.

On days when you simply can't be home on time, you may want to arrange with a neighbor or a professional dog-sitter to take your dog out,

You can usually stop housesoiling with remedial house-training and lots of praise for correct behavior.

says Kutsukos. Many people who work long hours now rely on dog-sitters to take their dogs out or walk them once or twice a day.

Go back to basic training. Most dogs that have started messing indoors simply need some remedial housetraining, says Kutsukos. So treat your dog like she's a puppy again. Take her outside when she wakes up, after naps, meals, and play sessions, and before bed. Stay with her, and when she does the deed, praise her. Inside, if she's nosing around for a choice spot, whisk her outside fast. Usually, your dog will quickly recall her old lessons and the problem will clear up fairly quickly.

Remind her who's in charge. Dogs occasionally urinate inside to mark their territory and assert their authority. Dogs with this type of attitude problem usually give other signs of dominance, like disobeying your orders. If you even suspect your dog is trying to get the upper hand, stop this fast with home obedience drills or obedience school. Asserting your authority will help her understand that you're the boss, and she won't feel the need to mark.

Keep her calm. Dogs are unhappy when their routine changes, such as moving house or when you're doing renovations, and may react by forgetting their house training. The best way to help your dog adjust to change is to give her lots of attention and exercise. And make sure she knows where she's supposed to relieve herself. As things calm down, she'll make every effort to do what she's supposed to, Kutsukos says.

CALL FOR HELP

When your dog suddenly starts messing indoors after years of good behavior, there's a good chance something is physically wrong.

Dogs with problems in the urinary system—anything from a bladder infection to kidney disease—will often get a sense of "urgency" that makes it impossible for them to hold their urine even for a few hours, says Janice M. Posnikoff, D.V.M., a veterinarian in private practice in Tustin, California. They may also have blood in the urine or need to urinate more often.

A number of other internal problems, including diabetes and Cushing's disease, can cause pets to lose bladder control, says Dr. Posnikoff. You should play it safe and take your dog for a checkup.

Jealousy

Your dog is just one of your special friends. He has to share your affection with your family, your close friends, and perhaps another dog or cat. However, he has a different perspective. You are his *only* best friend. Most dogs get used to this arrangement and live with it happily enough. But sometimes they get a little jealous, especially when the "competition" is a newcomer in the family—a baby, for example, or a new pet, says Trish King, animal behavior consultant for the Marin Humane Society in Marin County, California.

Some dogs show their displeasure by pushing in between you and whoever happens to be sitting too close. Or they get aggressive, growling and snapping at their rival. "Your dog sees it as his right to get your attention," King says.

Jealousy can cause real problems, both for you and your dog, says Joan Guertin, a dog trainer for Common Sense Dog Training in Branson, Missouri. "The longer it goes on, the more it intensifies," she says. "You need to correct it before it gets out of hand."

Give him some quality time. Dogs suffering jealousy's pangs can be remarkably persistent. They'll nuzzle your hand, rub against you, and follow you around the house like a shadow. It's a sad sight, but you should not give in to your dog every time he wants your total attention, King says. If you do, he'll continue to demand, and be anxious when he doesn't get it.

A better approach is to set aside some time several times a day when you'll positively lavish your dog with attention. After that, be prepared

This chocolate and white Border collie is learning to accept a baby in the family. Give your dog extra attention only when the object of his jealousy is near, and he will link his rival with feeling good.

to ignore him and go about your business. This will help your dog understand that he has to respect your limits, since he'll discover that he won't get attention when you're not prepared to give it to him.

Assert your authority. As long as you feel guilty about not giving your dog the attention he demands, he'll sense your weakness and keep pushing for more. This isn't the time to give in to his demands. Rather, it's time to make some demands of your own. Before you rub that insistent nose, make him sit or lie down. This will help him understand that you and not he is calling the shots. In addition, making your dog sit or lie down puts him in a lower, more subordinate position. "This helps lower his rank in the household and helps him understand that he is not the one in charge," says King.

If your dog ignores your commands, it's because he thinks he's in charge. Obedience classes will help you train your dog to listen to you.

Don't get involved. It's common for dogs to be jealous of other dogs that join the household. And when dogs get jealous, arguments often break out. Don't get involved when your dogs occasionally jockey for position, Guertin says. Instead, walk away without giving the jealous one any reaction. This will help him get the idea that jealous behavior simply doesn't pay off. Avoid punishing either dog, says Guertin, as this could result in a fight and further discourage the lower-ranking dog.

Help him see the pay-off. Dogs get jealous because they're afraid the interloper is going to steal your affections away from them. One way to turn their thinking around is to give them lots of attention only when the "new" person or pet is nearby, says King. If you have a new baby, for example, give your dog plenty of love and strokes when you're with your baby. The rest of the time, ignore him. Eventually, he'll come to link the baby with all the great attention he receives, and his jealousy will rapidly fade.

Keep things normal. As much as you can, try to treat your dog the same—take the same walks, give him the same amount of brushing, and so on—as you did before. Dogs are sticklers for routine, and they'll associate any disruptions in their lives with the newcomer. Keeping things predictable will help your dog understand that while the household may have changed, his expectations don't have to.

Teach him some social graces. Start preparing your dog, right from his puppy days, for potential changes in his life. That way, he'll be better able to cope with change when it arises. Encourage gregariousness by letting him play with other pups. Introduce him to visitors and let him spend time around children. And never let him try to dominate your attention, even when he's young. When he's used to being one of the crowd, he'll cope more easily with new arrivals who are also joining in.

Encourage new friendships. It's often hard for dogs to accept new people in the family, especially significant others who demand a lot of attention. One way to make sure everyone remains friends is to encourage new people in your life to take an active role in caring for your dog. It's hard for dogs to be jealous when the object of their disaffections is holding the leash or filling the food bowl each morning. You could also get the new person to give your dog the occasional special treat.

Like this young English bulldog, your puppy should start to learn the social graces as early as possible.

Possessiveness

For many dogs, nothing is more exciting than a game of catch. They'll tear after a ball or stick, grab it, and happily run back and drop it at your feet—then eagerly wait for you to throw it again. But there are times when dogs forget the rules. Rather than dropping the object, they refuse to give it up, as though to say, "It's mine, all mine." When you insist, they'll duck and dodge away—or drop their playful manner and give you an earnest stare, as though daring you to take it back. If this happens, it's time for a firm lesson in sharing.

"Dogs tend to become possessive over things they see as valuable resources, like toys, food, or rawhides," says Deborah Jones, Ph.D., a psychologist and dog trainer in Akron, Ohio. This behavior makes sense in the wild, where dogs roam in packs and possession is 100 per-cent of the law. But even in the wild there's one simple rule: No dog will take a possession from another dog that's higher in the pecking order.

What your dog is forgetting is that in your family, you're the leader, with all the rights that position confers. When your dog holds onto a toy and won't give it back, he's essentially challenging your authority, and that can lead to aggression and other problems, says Trish King, an animal behavior consultant for the Marin Humane Society in Marin, California.

Whether your dog is a puppy or an adult, there's no excuse for acting possessive and pushing around the human members of the family, King says. He needs to learn how to share and, more important, how to respect your authority. Here are a few ways to turn him around.

Overwhelm his expectations. Since dogs get possessive over what they think are valuable resources, you can devalue these objects simply by providing more of them, King says. Instead of giving him just one tennis ball, for example, give him five or six. He'll be so overwhelmed with his riches that he probably won't object when you take one or two away, even when they happen to be the ones he's playing with.

Get rid of temptation. Sometimes a dog becomes obsessed with one toy or object that he prizes above all others, and he'll do anything—including ignoring your commands—to keep from giving it up. Wait for a quiet moment to grab the toy and throw it away. Don't use force to get your dog to give up his toy because he may get upset and you could get bitten. Remov-

POOCH PUZZLER

Why do dogs bury bones?

After making a big kill, wolves will bury large pieces of meat to provide future meals. They bury the meat in private so that others in the pack won't slip over and dig it up on the sly.

Dogs are a long way from their wolfish ancestors, but the burying habit survives. Dogs don't bury food—after all, they know where their next meal is coming from—but they do bury toys, tennis balls, and especially bones. They know that once a bone is underground, no other pets (or people) will steal it.

BREED SPECIFIC

All of the retrieving breeds, such as Labrador retrievers, golden retrievers, flat-coated retrievers, and Chesapeake Bay retrievers, are notoriously possessive because they were bred to grab hold of their "prey" and not let go until they made it back to their owner.

ing temptation is much easier than making your dog overcome it, and once his favorite toy is out of the way, he's much less likely to be possessive or challenging, says Dr. Jones.

Teach him to let go. After "sit," "stay," and "come," the command "drop it" is one of the most important lessons your dog will learn. Not only is it helpful for reducing possessive behavior and teaching obedience, but it will also help get things like fast-food wrappers or sharp objects out of his mouth before he has a chance to swallow them.

It's an easy command to teach. Start by saying "drop it" when your dog has nothing in his mouth, and immediately give him a treat. Do this several times a day for a few days. Then give the command when he has something in his mouth—preferably an object he's interested in, but not deeply attached to. When he drops it, give him a treat and a lot of praise. If you keep doing this he will soon learn that following orders sometimes brings tasty rewards, and he'll be much less likely to be grabby and belligerent.

Break his meal-time concentration. Nearly all dogs are extremely possessive of their food, sometimes to the point that they'll growl

or snap when people walk by. One way to change their attitude is to take away their food bowl for a while. Spread the food on the grass one day and on a sheet of newspaper the next. Keep feeding your dog in different places with his food spread out in different ways. By stopping him from focusing on the source of his pleasure—the food bowl itself—he'll be less aggressive about protecting what he mistakenly perceives as his.

Another way to stop meal-time possessiveness is to hand-feed your dog his dinner sometimes, one piece of kibble at a time, says Dr. Jones. This will cause him to associate your hands with "getting" rather than "taking away," she explains. And it strengthens your position as the dominant member of the family who controls what and when he eats. Once he understands these rules, he'll welcome your authority instead of rebelling against it.

This Irish terrier is learning to "drop it." He has dropped his toy to get the treat in his owner's hand.

Separation Anxiety

The emotional bond that dogs form with their owners can be extraordinarily intense. They follow us around the house, sleep on the floor by the bed, and watch anxiously when we walk out the door without them. The depth of their dedication is wonderful—it's one of the reasons people love dogs so much. But for some dogs, their attachment is so intense that they simply can't bear to have their owners out of sight and will go slightly crazy whenever they're left alone. Experts refer to this condition as separation anxiety.

When their owners leave the house, dogs with separation anxiety do everything they can to cope with their fear. Unfortunately, their way of coping usually involves such things as endless barking, destroying shoes, furniture, and other belongings, or jumping over fences or through plate glass windows, says Steven Appelbaum, an animal behaviorist in Northridge, California.

Like humans, dogs are social animals. "It's stressful to them to be separated from other creatures," says Patricia McConnell, Ph.D., a certified applied animal behaviorist in Black Earth, Wisconsin. Of course, most dogs deal with their stress in calmer, less destructive ways—usually by going to sleep or playing with their toys. But for dogs with separation anxiety—who either never got used to being alone when they were young or had some traumatic experience— sleep is not an option. All they want is to work off their fear—and to have their owner home.

It doesn't do any good to punish dogs with this problem, says Appelbaum. Instead, help your dog learn that being alone isn't the same thing as being abandoned.

Forget the fond farewells. When you know your dog is frightened, it's hard to walk out the door without giving him an emotional goodbye, or to come back home without giving him a huge welcome. But it's not a good idea to make a big deal out of arrivals and departures, says Appelbaum. It teaches your dog to attach too much importance to your comings and goings, when what you want him to do is take them for granted. A better strategy is to ignore your dog totally for about 10 minutes before you leave the house and after you return. When he sees that you're not all shook up, he'll be more likely to take his cue from you.

Keep him occupied. Find a way to take his mind off his fear. One of the best things you can do is leave plenty of toys where he can get them, says Dr. McConnell. A favorite choice is a hollow bone or a hollow Kong brand toy, with cavities you can fill with cheese or peanut butter. Most dogs will happily spend hours trying to get out all the goodies stuffed inside.

BREED SPECIFIC

Bred to spend a lot of time with humans, toy breeds, such as Lhasa apsos and Boston terriers, and sporting dogs, such as golden and Labrador retrievers, tend to get anxious when they're left alone.

Another way to keep his mind occupied is to engage him in a treasure hunt. Stash some of his food around the house—in places he can reach, but will have to hunt out, like behind a chair or under a magazine. His nose will soon let him know that something special's going on. Do this at the same time as you begin making the signs that let your dog know you're about to leave, such as picking up your keys or walking to the door. Don't leave the house the first few times you organize a treasure hunt until he shows no anxiety when you make the signs you're leaving. He may eventually associate your leaving with fun times, or at least won't be upset when you leave. Instead, he'll be occupied with the hunt and won't become too anxious while you're away.

A Kong toy stuffed with edible treats will keep this Staffordshire bull terrier entertained for hours.

Give a little less pampering. There's nothing wrong with giving your dog plenty of attention, but you don't want to overdo it with dogs that are already anxious, says Dr. McConnell. Giving too much attention makes them crave your company even more, which can cause problems when you're not there. Discourage your dog from spending all his time at your feet or following you around, and don't give him attention just because he's near. What you want is for him to welcome your attention, but not go crazy when it isn't forthcoming.

Wear him out. Tired dogs are less likely to be fearful dogs, so it's worth tiring your dog out before you leave the house. "Exercise is a wonderful sedative," says Dr. McConnell.

Find him a friend. Some dogs never get entirely used to being alone. If you can't spend time at home during the day, you may want to have a pet sitter come in once a day. Or you can enroll your dog in doggy day care, where he'll get some extra company, says Appelbaum. Although it won't give him the company he really wants—yours—it will help keep him occupied.

Call in the experts. If your dog doesn't respond to any of these techniques, consider getting some professional help from an animal trainer. Have your dog checked out by your vet to make sure that pain or illness are not causing him stress. You could also help increase his confidence by enrolling him in obedience classes.

After an energetic session of play, this golden retriever will be happy to sleep when his owner goes out.

Advisers

KEN ABRAMS, D.V.M., is a veterinary ophthalmologist in private practice in Warwick, Rhode Island.

LOWELL ACKERMAN, D.V.M., Ph.D., is a veterinary dermatologist in private practice in Mesa, Arizona, and author of *Skin and Haircoat Problems in Dogs*.

JOAN E. ANTLE, D.V.M., is a veterinarian in private practice in Cleveland, Ohio.

STEVEN APPELBAUM is an animal behaviorist in Northridge, California.

SUSAN BONHOWER is a Newfoundland breeder in Cornwall, Ontario, Canada.

PETER BORCHELT, Ph.D., is a certified applied animal behaviorist at Animal Behavior Associates in Brooklyn, New York.

MARY R. BURCH, Ph.D., is a certified applied animal behaviorist in Tallahassee, Florida.

WILLIAM E. CAMPBELL is a dog behavior consultant in Grants Pass, Oregon, and author of *Behavior Problems in Dogs*.

RON CARSTEN, D.V.M., is a veterinarian in private practice in Glenwood Springs, Colorado.

CRAIG N. CARTER, D.V.M., Ph.D., is head of epidemiology at the Texas Veterinary Medical Diagnostic Laboratories at Texas A&M University in College Station.

MERRY CRIMI, D.V.M., is a veterinarian in private practice in Portland, Oregon.

BERNARDINE CRUZ, D.V.M., is a veterinarian in private practice in Laguna Hills, California.

L. R. DANIEL, D.V.M., is a veterinarian in private practice in Covington, Louisiana.

KATHY DIAMOND DAVIS is a dog trainer in Oklahoma City.

EDMUND DOROSZ, D.V.M., is a veterinarian in private practice in Ft. Macleod, Alberta, Canada.

ROBIN DOWNING, D.V.M., is a veterinarian in private practice in Windsor, Colorado.

MICHAEL DRYDEN, D.V.M., Ph.D., is associate professor of veterinary parasitology at Kansas State University's College of Veterinary Medicine in Manhattan.

GREGG DUPONT, D.V.M., is a veterinarian in private practice in Seattle.

PETER EEG, D.V.M., is a veterinarian in private practice in Poolesville, Maryland.

DANIEL Q. ESTEP, Ph.D., is a certified applied animal behaviorist in Littleton, Colorado.

NICK A. FABOR, D.V.M., is a veterinary ophthalmologist at the School of Veterinary Medicine at the University of California, Davis.

BRAD FENWICK, D.V.M., is from the department of clinical sciences at Kansas State University's College of Veterinary Medicine in Manhattan.

ROBERT FLECKER, D.V.M., is a veterinarian in private practice in Tualatin, Oregon.

WILLIAM J. FORTNEY, D.V.M., is a veterinarian in the department of clinical sciences at Kansas State University's College of Veterinary Medicine in Manhattan.

EILEEN GABRIEL is a professional dog groomer in Yorktown Heights, New York.

KATHY GAUGHAN, D.V.M., is assistant professor in the department of clinical sciences at Kansas State University's College of Veterinary Medicine in Manhattan.

JOHN GIANNONE, D.V.M., is a veterinarian in private practice in Yorktown Heights, New York.

PAUL GIGLIOTTI, D.V.M., is a veterinarian in private practice in Cleveland, Ohio.

STUART GLUCKMAN, D.V.M., is a veterinarian in private practice in Mendon, New York.

LINDA GOODLOE, Ph.D., is a certified applied animal behaviorist in New York City.

JOAN GUERTIN is a dog trainer for Common Sense Dog Training in Branson, Missouri.

STEVE HANSEN, D.V.M., is a veterinary toxicologist and director of the ASPCA National Animal Poison Control Center in Urbana, Illinois.

KENNETH HARKIN, D.V.M., is assistant professor in the department of clinical sciences at Kansas State University's College of Veterinary Medicine in Manhattan.

WAYNE HUNTHAUSEN, D.V.M., is an animal behavior consultant in Kansas City.

HILARY JACKSON, B.V.M.&S., is assistant professor of dermatology at North Carolina State University College of Veterinary Medicine in Raleigh.

DENNIS JENSEN, D.V.M., is a veterinarian in private practice in Houston, Texas.

DEBORAH JONES, Ph.D., is a psychologist and dog trainer in Akron, Ohio.

LAUREL KADDATZ, D.V.M., is a veterinarian in private practice in Fairport, New York.
STEVEN KASANOFSKY, D.V.M., is a veterinarian in private practice in New York City.
TRISH KING is an animal behavior consultant for the Marin Humane Society in Marin County, California.
ROBIN KOVARY is a dog trainer, behavioral consultant, and director of the American Dog Trainer's Network in New York City.
JEANNENE KUTSUKOS is a dog trainer at Pro Dog Training in Springfield, Illinois.

HARRIET LEDERMAN, V.M.D., is a veterinarian in private practice in Millburn, New Jersey.
DARYL B. LEU, D.V.M., is a veterinarian with a dermatology referral practice in Portland, Oregon.
THOMAS LEWIS, D.V.M., is a veterinarian in private practice in Mesa, Arizona.

PATRICIA MCCONNELL, Ph.D., is a certified animal behaviorist in Black Earth, Wisconsin.
TERRY MCCOY, D.V.M., is a veterinarian in private practice in Corvallis, Oregon.
KAREN MATEYAK, D.V.M., is a veterinarian in private practice in Brooklyn, New York.
MICHAEL MATZ, D.V.M., is a veterinary internal medicine specialist in Tucson, Arizona.
CARI MAYER is a dog groomer in Greenwich, Connecticut.
PATRICK MELESE, D.V.M., is a certified applied animal behaviorist in San Diego.
JILLIAN MESNICK, D.V.M., is a veterinarian in private practice in Mayfield Village, Ohio.
WILLIAM H. MILLER JR., V.M.D., is professor of dermatology at Cornell University's College of Veterinary Medicine in Ithaca, New York.
DAVE MONZO is from Canine Partners for Life in Cochranville, Pennsylvania.

CAROLINE NOTHWANGER, D.V.M., is a veterinarian in private practice in Fairfax, Virginia.
JAMES NOXON, D.V.M., is staff dermatologist at the Veterinary Teaching College of Iowa State University in Ames.

DANIELA ORTNER is an animal behaviorist in Los Angeles.

PAUL D. PION, D.V.M., is a veterinary cardiologist in private practice in Sacramento, California, and co-founder of the Veterinary Information Network.

JANICE M. POSNIKOFF, D.V.M., is a veterinarian in private practice in Tustin, California.

ROBERT RIDLEY, D.V.M., Ph.D., is professor of pathology at Kansas State University's College of Veterinary Medicine in Manhattan.
GENE RIVERS, D.V.M., is a veterinarian in private practice in Seattle.
JAMES ROSS, D.V.M., is chair of the department of clinical sciences at Tufts University School of Veterinary Medicine in North Grafton, Massachusetts.
RICHARD J. ROSSMAN, D.V.M., is a veterinarian in private practice in Glenview, Illinois.

JODY SANDLER, D.V.M., is director of veterinary services for Guiding Eyes for the Blind in Yorktown Heights, New York.
ALLEN SCHOEN, D.V.M., is a veterinarian in private practice in Sherman, Connecticut.
RANCE SELLON, D.V.M., is assistant professor in the department of veterinary clinical sciences at Washington State University in Pullman.
AMY SHOJA is author of *Competability: A Practical Guide to Building a Peaceable Kingdom between Dogs and Cats.*
BARBARA S. SIMPSON, D.V.M., Ph.D., is a certified applied animal behaviorist in Southern Pines, North Carolina.

PATRICK TATE, D.V.M., is a veterinarian in private practice in St. Louis, Missouri.

SHELLY VADEN, D.V.M., is associate professor of internal medicine at North Carolina State University's College of Veterinary Medicine in Raleigh.
DIANE VAN TINE, D.V.M., is a veterinarian in private practice in Conifor, Colorado.

TAYLOR WALLACE, D.V.M., is a veterinarian in private practice in Seattle.
ROBERT WIGGS, D.V.M., is a veterinarian in private practice in Dallas, Texas.
CHRISTINE WILFORD, D.V.M., is a veterinarian in private practice in Seattle.
LORI A. WISE, D.V.M., is a veterinarian in private practice in Wheat Ridge, Colorado.
JAN WOLF, D.V.M., is a veterinarian in private practice in Kenosha, Wisconsin.
JERRY WOODFIELD, D.V.M., is a veterinary cardiologist in private practice in Seattle.
SUSAN G. WYNN, D.V.M., is a veterinarian in private practice in Marietta, Georgia.

Index

Underscored pages references indicate boxed text. *Italic* references indicate illustrations.

Acknowledgments and Credits

The publisher would like to thank the following people for their assistance in the preparation of this book:

Trudie Craig; Robert Coupe; Gillian Hewitt; Pets International; RSPCA; St Ives Purr-fect Pets; Selene Yeager; Clare Macken; Bethan Jones.

Special thanks to all the people who kindly brought their dogs in for photo shoots.

ILLUSTRATION AND PHOTOGRAPH CREDITS (t=top, b=bottom, l=left, r=right, c=center, F=front, C=cover, B=back). All photographs are copyright to the sources listed below.

Ad-Libitum: Stuart Bowey, ic, vib, viict, 2b, 5b, 7b, 13b, 14b, 15c, 17t, 18b, 21t, 21c, 21b, 26t, 27b, 31b, 33b, 36b, 37t, 41b, 44b, 45t, 46b, 47t, 48b, 49b, 50b, 54b, 55b, 58t, 60b, 60t, 61t, 62b, 63t, 65b, 66t, 69b, 71b, 73b, 74b, 77t, 80b, 84bl, 84br, 85b, 86b, 88t, 92t, 93bl, 93br, 93cl, 93cr, 94cb, 96b, 98t, 99b, 101b, 102b, 103b, 106b, 108b, 109b, 114b, 116b, 117b, 120b, 123b, 124b, 126b, 129b, 130t, 138b, 139b, 140b, 141b, 143tc, 143tc, 143tl, 143tl, 143tr, 143tr, 144b, 146t, 148b, 150bl, 151tr, 151tr, 154t, 157b, 159b, 159t, BCb, BCr.

Auscape International: 10t, 76b, Bernie-COGIS, 1c; COGIS, 67b; Fleury-COGIS, 136b; Francais-COGIS, 28c,

155c; Gehlhar-COGIS, 115t; Hermeline/COGIS, 68c, 105b; Isabelle Francais-COGIS, 146b; Jean-Michel Labat, 118b, 144t, BCltc; Jean-Paul Ferrero, 4b; Labat-COGIS, iic; Labat/Lanceau/Cogis, 75b; Lanceau-COGIS, 111t, 124t, 152b; Varin/COGIS, 134c.

Behling & Johnson: Norvia Behling, viiib, 127t.

Bill Bachman and Associates: Bill Bachman, 3t, 5t, 64b, 112c, 137t, 148t, 153t, BClt, BClbc.

Bruce Coleman Ltd: Hans Reinhard, 142b.

Graham Meadows Photography: Graham Meadows, 30c, 133b.

Dennis Mosner: FC.

Robert Harding Picture Library: OMH Black, 95t.

Ron Kimball Studios: Ron Kimball, 97t.

Stock Photos: Paul Barton, 121t.

The Image Bank: viicb, 11c, 34c, 31t, 32t, 91c, 118t.

Illustrations: Virginia Gray, 9c, 23b, 61b, 78b, 79c, 90t, 104b, 110b, 131b. Chris Wilson/Merilake, 16b, 35t, 39t, 39b, 40b, 43t, 52t, 53t, 56t, 56b, 70b, 81c, 125b.